ALSO BY BUSTER OLNEY

The Last Night of the Yankee Dynasty:
The Game, the Team, and the Cost of Greatness

How
Lucky
You Can Be

How Lucky You Can Be

THE STORY OF COACH DON MEYER

BUSTER OLNEY

Ballantine Books | New York

Published in the United States by ESPN Books, an imprint of ESPN, Inc., New York,
and Ballantine Books, an imprint of The Random House Publishing Group,
a division of Random House, Inc., New York.

BALLANTINE and colophon are registered trademarks of Random House, Inc.
The ESPN Books name and logo are registered trademarks of ESPN, Inc.

Library of Congress Cataloging-in-Publication Data
Olney, Buster.
How lucky you can be : the story of Coach Don Meyer / Buster Olney.
p.   cm.
ISBN 978-0-345-52411-9 (hardcover : alk. paper)
eBook ISBN 978-0-345-52413-3
1. Meyer, Don, 1944–   2. Basketball—Coaching.   I. Title.
GV885.3.O56 2010
796.323092—dc22   2010030200
[B}

Printed in the United States of America [on acid-free paper]

www.ballantinebooks.com
www.espnbooks.com

2 4 6 8 9 7 5 3 1

Design by R. Bull

For Amelia
Good morning to you . . .

How
Lucky
You Can Be

CHAPTER 1

The body was on the floor and except for the rise and fall of the chest, there was no movement. The legs were tilted upward onto the seat of a chair. This is what Brenda Dreyer saw in the middle of her office on the afternoon of September 5, 2008.

She stepped from the room, pulled out her cell phone, and punched in numbers. It was three o'clock in Aberdeen, South Dakota.

"Coach is here," she said into the phone in a low voice. "He's sleeping. Do you want me to wake him?"

"No," said Randy Baruth, the assistant men's basketball coach at Northern State University. "Let him sleep. As long as he's ready to go by four, that's fine."

Outside of Dreyer's office, the Northern State campus was bustling on this first Friday of the school year. A class of freshmen found their way around, asking the same questions that the older students had asked before them. Students registered for classes and flocked to the bookstore to buy texts. Old friendships were renewed.

By tradition, on the first Friday of each school year, members of the men's basketball team would drive forty miles to a nearby hunting lodge off campus, a retreat designed to give the incoming freshmen a chance to assimilate. Through stories, a cookout, and games, the Wolves' players and coaches would learn more about one another, and about themselves. This was a day of rebirth.

The caravan of coaches and players was scheduled to leave at four. But Don Meyer, the sixty-three-year-old head basketball coach at Northern State—a man eleven wins shy of Bob Knight's NCAA men's record for most wins in history—was dead asleep, in one of the handful of spots on campus where he took naps in the middle of the day, lying on his back, baseball cap tilted over his eyes, feet propped on a chair.

He had been an early riser his entire life. Having grown up on a Nebraska farm with a taskmaster father, Meyer tended to wake at four or five A.M., work through the morning, and then tire easily in the middle of the afternoon.

Coaching made his schedule that much more exhausting. Recruiting in the Dakotas and other western states was done by car, in drives measured in hours rather than miles. And because Northern State's athletic programs shared one gymnasium in the middle of the South Dakota winter, the practices for the men's basketball team were often held at six A.M. Some days Meyer and an assistant would drive most of the night and then go straight to practice. Sleeping in until seven A.M. or later was not an option, and Meyer didn't drink coffee or caffeinated soda.

The weariness was so constant that he often slipped catnaps into his schedule.

But he couldn't do that in his office, because even in September, before the team was practicing every morning, his day could be overrun by phone calls and emails and videotapes. The door to Meyer's office was kept open all day. A windowless square ten feet by ten feet, built with facing cement blocks and drywall, Meyer's office could've been confused for a place of solitary confinement—save for the way the place was decorated and the nonstop human traffic. Other coaches walked through Meyer's office to get from the main lobby to their offices. Basketball players came to check in by signing the blue notebook that rested on a bookshelf opposite his desk. Friends stopped by just to chat. Meyer liked having his office in the middle of everything.

His walls were covered with pictures and posters and placards containing mantras or memories. Coaching legend John Wooden, a longtime friend of Meyer's, commanded the most space, with his gold pyramid of success and framed pictures of Wooden from the day he flew into Aberdeen to work Meyer's annual coaching clinic. Meyer had a sign, colored in UCLA gold, that was filled with words that had been given to Wooden by his father:

Don't Whine. Don't Complain. Don't Make Excuses.

A plaque for the national championship team that Meyer coached in 1986 at David Lipscomb College hung on one wall. File cabinets and boxes were stacked in a corner, leaving just enough room for Meyer to turn one hundred and eighty degrees in his black swivel chair and type into his computer.

But because his office was the superhighway of the Northern State gym, he couldn't nap there without being interrupted. So Meyer would escape to three or four different spots on campus

Don Meyer and John Wooden at a coaching clinic in 1994.

where he could sit, lower the bill of his cap, and doze. The Hall of Fame room at the Barnett Center. The office of Harry Jasinski, the jocular eighty-one-year-old professor emeritus. The office of Brenda Dreyer, Northern State's director of university relations, where she found him on this day with his feet propped up.

Eventually, Meyer stirred and, seeing Dreyer, tried to get up. But his feet got tangled with the chair and he grasped at Dreyer's extended hand, both of them laughing at his awkwardness. "You dope," Dreyer said. Finally, he rose.

Meyer was six foot two, a former college pitcher and basketball player. He had lost most of his hair in early adulthood, and because his default expression was a concentrated frown, with his right eyebrow arched, those who met Meyer initially thought he was humorless, a notion shattered as soon as they came to recognize his droll sarcasm and love of jokes. Like this one, which he heard from Wooden and repeated often:

A cowboy comes in off the hot trail, hot and dusty from the cattle drive, and struts into a bar. He is all business, John Wayne–tough, and he announces to everyone in the bar, "My horse is outside, and nobody better take it, or else I'll have to do what I done did down in Texas."

He orders a sarsaparilla, the place is dead quiet, and the bartender leans forward and quietly asks, "What was it that you done did down in Texas?"

"Walk," the cowboy says.

Meyer left the administration building and returned to his office, and in the last minutes before the drive to the hunting lodge, he filled in the day planner that ranked, in its importance to him, somewhere among air and water.

The plan was for Randy Baruth, the assistant coach, to drive at the head of the caravan. When Baruth had begun as Meyer's assistant coach at Northern State, Meyer usually started at the wheel when they took their hours-long recruiting trips together. But Baruth could see that Meyer sometimes struggled to stay awake on long drives, especially later in the day, and Meyer told Baruth stories about waking up on the road and not remembering how he got to where he was; so, in time, Baruth did almost all of the driving whenever they traveled together.

Once, in Baruth's second year working for Meyer, the Wolves recruited a kid who lived in Crosby, North Dakota—about sixteen miles from the U.S.-Canada border, and some four hundred miles from Northern State University. Meyer and Baruth were scheduled to visit with the player at about ten A.M., and Baruth figured that they would drive much of the route the night before the meeting, check in to a hotel, and then finish the drive the next morning. But Meyer insisted on leaving at two A.M. and driving straight through the night. Baruth was furious at Meyer's stubbornness over not spending money to get a hotel room, but this was Meyer's way. His players had always joked about how cheap he was. If the choice came down to paying twenty-nine dollars for a hotel room and getting a decent night's sleep or pushing through, Meyer would keep driving. "That's the stupidest thing I ever heard of," Baruth said. "You're driving." An hour into the trip, Baruth looked over and could see that Meyer was having difficulty staying awake; fuming, Baruth drove the rest of the way to Crosby, and all the way back.

Baruth figured he would be at the wheel, even on the short trip to the retreat. The players were ready to leave at four P.M., as scheduled. But Baruth was behind in his work; he needed to copy some materials to send to a recruit. Finally, Baruth told Meyer, "Hey, Coach, I'll just meet you out there."

The drive wasn't long, just forty minutes. The team's caravan of six cars left the parking lot of the Barnett Center a little after four o'clock, the cars packed with sleeping bags and food to grill. Alone in the lead, in a four-door Toyota Prius bought for its efficient gas mileage, was Don Meyer. Husband to Carmen Meyer for forty-one years. Father of three. Grandfather of eight.

The lodge was easy enough to get to, a left turn and then some rights. After a mile on Melgaard Road, a left turn onto South Dakota Road 281—and then straight into the horizon. Through a windshield, the prairie sky looked like a blue semicircle set upon the land. Harvest was just weeks away, and rows and rows of corn filled the fields on both sides of the road. Old-fashioned telephone poles ran parallel to State Road 281, wooden crosses holding up double strands of wires.

They passed the Brown County Rifle Range on their right, and Kamen Equipment on their left, two of the few real landmarks in Brown County. Round bales were scattered across fields, rising like dunes in a desert. In some fields, the round bales were stacked three high—the farmer's pyramid of success—to keep them out of the pools of water that often collected on South Dakota's flat fields. In another couple of months, these plains would be filled so thick with snow geese and Canada geese that it would look as if you could walk across entire fields while only stepping on the backs of the birds.

The caravan, with the cars close together, crossed into Spink County, but the only way they would know the difference was by the sign. The only thing modern out there was the glimmering harvesting equipment, parked in front of farmhouses with peeling paint.

Twenty-one miles down the road there was a sign that pointed in three directions. Meyer turned west onto South Dakota Highway 20, toward Northville, the other cars following.

Kyle Schwan, one of the team's seniors, was driving the fifth car in line, chatting with a carful of teammates. Bojan Todorovic, sitting directly behind Schwan, started to fall asleep, lulled by the landscape. They passed Northville's cemetery.

There were no tall trees cutting into the landscape, because of centuries of wind; there were just rows of cottonwood, mostly no more than twenty-five feet high and mostly in seeded lines to mark property boundaries or to just provide a little cover from the relentless prairie gusts. Herds of Black Angus cattle were sprinkled on the landscape; the cattle tilted their heads down, pulling at the grass with their mouths, flicking at flies with their tails. The wind blew, as it almost always does here—an easy 10 mph on this day, just enough to make the fields of wheat and the corn stalks ripple.

Highway 20 rose and fell gently between more cornfields, and every quarter mile, there were small inlets into the fields, used by the harvesters. The caravan drove into the afternoon sun. It was sixty-three degrees. Meyer looked for the turnoff.

Brett Newton, a sophomore guard on the Northern State team, was seated in the car second in line in the caravan, directly behind Meyer. He saw the coach's car begin to drift across Highway 20, over both yellow lines. And he saw a semi, hauling a trailer, barreling in the other direction, eastbound. Meyer's car and the semi were both moving about 55 mph, right at each other.

In an instant, the thought passed through Newton's mind that Meyer would surely turn his wheel and pull his car back on track. "Coach!" Newton shouted. "Coach!"

Meyer's car continued to drift into the eastbound lane. Now the driver's side wheels were well across the yellow lines, taking up almost half of the lane just fifteen feet wide.

The left front side of Meyer's car smashed into the left front of the semi, disappearing briefly into a cloud of metal, rubber, plastic, and glass. One player would later say it looked like something out of a Hollywood action movie. Except this was real life. This was Coach Meyer.

The impact of the collision drove the front of Meyer's car an inch into the asphalt. The tires exploded, and two doors from Meyer's car were launched straight into the air; one of them flew over the second car in the Northern State caravan. Meyer's tire was thrown to the rear by the collision, into the path of the oncoming cars. The body of Meyer's car spun counterclockwise, bouncing off the body of the truck.

Meyer's car twisted across the highway, probably twice, and came to rest on the side of the road, on a twelve-foot embankment, facing east, rather than west. The second and third cars in the caravan rolled to a stop near Meyer's car, off the side of the road.

Tramel Barnes, a freshman, drove the fourth car in the caravan; he saw the debris from the collision shoot into the air. Suddenly, the front corner of the semi rumbled directly at him. He felt the back end of his car get lifted up and knocked to the side; the glancing blow from the truck ripped his car off its back axle and nudged the back end to the shoulder.

Bojan Todorovic, riding behind Kyle Schwan in the backseat of the fifth car, was still asleep when Meyer hit the semi, but was jarred awake when Schwan instinctively tapped his brake at the sight of the collision. Bojan was among the five players stuffed into Schwan's four-door Honda; Bojan was six foot nine and there were three players in the car taller than him.

Bojan looked up and saw the grille of the semi barreling directly at him, and he screamed out. Schwan saw the front of the truck too, and slammed his right foot onto the gas pedal and turned the wheel hard to his right, trying to get out of the path of the truck. He braced for impact, and heard a distinct sound directly behind him: *Vwoomp!* Bojan heard it too.

It was the sound of the front corner of a semi clipping off the casing of the back light of a Honda.

Schwan's car was otherwise intact and rocketed over the shoulder and down a short embankment before rolling to a stop. The semi rolled across the westbound lane of Highway 20, barreling over the shoulder and then sinking into the grassy apron alongside the highway, facing north.

Everything stopped. A moment of silence. And then car doors started opening, with the players jumping out and running toward Meyer's car.

Matt Hammer, the driver in the last car in the caravan, had played for Meyer for four years before returning to Northern State University to serve as a graduate assistant coach. Now, as Hammer burst out of his car and started running down Highway 20 toward the remains of Meyer's car, he fought the fear that the man who had influenced his life more than anyone other than his own father was already dead.

CHAPTER 2

"Just start running!"

Don Meyer's angry words ricocheted off the walls of the gym at David Lipscomb College* in Nashville, Tennessee. This was supposed to be a routine basketball practice in the fall of 1989. But Meyer was furious about something and he was determined to punish the players, and they didn't know why. The players lined up on the baseline underneath one basket, Meyer blew a whistle, and they started sprinting full-speed to the other baseline and back. Up and back. Up and back. Up and back. Up and back.

Five minutes elapsed. Ten.

*Renamed David Lipscomb University in 1988, and then Lipscomb University in 2005.

Breathlessness turned into weariness for the players. In that moment, the youngest feared that if they stopped running they might be sent home for good. The seniors, like Wade Tomlinson and Philip Hutcheson, had a different perspective. Meyer had seemed tense all fall, probably because David Lipscomb was ranked number one in the country in NAIA's preseason poll.

Meyer's teams usually won eighty percent of their games. He had coached Lipscomb to a national title in 1986, and while he was not a household name, he was a giant in the coaching world; Meyer had operated the largest summer camps in the country, he had hosted well-attended coaching clinics that featured the likes of Bobby Knight and Pat Summitt, and Meyer had produced a popular series of instructional videos. But Meyer had never trusted success, and fretted that either he or the players might get soft mentally, so he tended to push his players even harder when his team was doing well.

On this day, somebody on the team might have broken a rule, some players thought, but they also assumed Meyer was trying to make a larger point. Maybe he thought the team wasn't focused. Maybe he thought there was too much selfishness in the ranks of the players. Maybe he meant to test their will, their toughness. He always had a larger point.

Fifteen minutes went by; up and back, up and back. Twenty minutes. Up and back.

Meyer shouted at them as they ran, yelling reminders of what they needed to do in school, what they needed to do for the team, what they needed to do for their teammates.

The David Lipscomb basketball players were in excellent physical condition, but running that hard, with a constant change of direction, was not something they were trained to do. Some players began getting sick, stepping off the court to throw up.

Thirty minutes. Tomlinson began shouting at the others, encouraging, cajoling. "Don't let him break you!" he shouted.

After forty-five minutes, the misery ended. Meyer informed them that one of their teammates had failed to show up for an English class. A selfish decision by one of them, he said, reflected on all of them. They needed to believe in the concept of serving others. He had made the larger point emphatically.

Meyer's drill-sergeant voice seemed custom-made for a gymnasium. Thousands of fans could be screaming or cheering, a referee's whistle blowing, scoreboard buzzers sounding, and yet Meyer's voice had such construction—built on a foundation of exasperation and anger and incredulity, roofed by just the right dab of sarcasm—that it rose above all other sounds. The hardwood of the basketball floor and acoustics of the small gymnasiums where he coached served him like a bullhorn.

During games, his shouted admonitions left no doubt for the fans within a zip code or two which of his players had just transgressed and precisely what their mistakes had been. He could be even harder on players in practice, stopping the action to challenge his players' decision making, their execution, their standing as young men who theoretically had a chance to be productive members of society. At the moment Meyer was yelling, that possibility was very much in doubt.

"PHILIP! WHAT ARE YOU THINKING!!?"

"WADE! WAS THAT A GOOD SHOT??!"

"HEY, KYLE—YOU'RE NOT PLAYING
FOR DADDY ANYMORE!!"

Matt Hammer played for Meyer for four years, and during one game, he had been unnecessarily aggressive on defense and committed a silly foul. At the exact instant the opposing player prepared to shoot free throws, in the brief quiet of the gym, Meyer

Meyer on the sidelines at Northern State University.

yelled at Hammer: *"Hey, Matt—you want to guard his free throws too??!!"* Hammer could hear the fans chuckling at his expense.

Meyer stalked the sidelines in front of his bench, his right eyebrow angled high, like that of a parent listening to his kid's excuse about why the garbage wasn't taken out. Meyer followed the action up and down the court, like a border collie locked in on the movement of sheep. Sometimes, if one of his own players got ready to take a shot directly in front of Meyer, he would say loud enough for the player to hear, *"Nail it!"* Sometimes, Hammer said, it felt like he was right inside your ear.

In Meyer's first decades as coach, he would often pause in front of a team manager seated on the bench to give him a couple of words about some flaw that he was seeing on the floor, and the manager would fill out page after page of these kinds of notes. Maybe somebody didn't block out, or failed to raise the ball to his chin in the triple-threat position that Meyer demanded from his players. Later, Meyer carried a digital tape recorder along the sidelines and took care of the note-taking himself, speaking directly into the recorder and transcribing those notes after the game.

He could command any room with his voice and his knowledge. But when players first got to know Meyer, their one-on-one conversations could be a much different experience.

He didn't really use verbal salutations, and there was no preamble or contextual clue; he'd just follow the tangents of his mind. His own daughters had reminded him many times, with proper respect and humor, that he was socially clueless. Meyer once called Vanderbilt baseball coach Tim Corbin, someone whom he had never met before. "Is this Coach Corbin?" Meyer asked abruptly. "This is Don Meyer. How did you turn your program around?"

He tended to mumble in one-on-one talk, or focus on something else as he talked to a player—maybe something on the computer screen in front of him, or a book, or maybe words he was writing. Sometimes players weren't really sure whether he was listening; Philip Hutcheson wondered if Meyer might be a little hard of hearing. A player could be explaining some classroom situation, and Meyer would look down, writing notes that had nothing to do with what the player was talking about. Or he might suddenly reach for the digital recorder and utter a couple of words—*"Wooden drill"*—a reminder of something that had flashed into his brain. It didn't help that for those meeting him for the first time—such as his youngest players—he initially seemed humorless, unsmiling.

Steve Smiley, a freshman at Northern State University, walked into Meyer's office with a teammate to meet him in the fall of 1999. There was no hello; Meyer didn't do hellos. The first words Meyer said to him were, "Do you have a notebook and pen?"

Meyer spoke for twenty minutes without looking at Smiley and his teammate. As he finished, Meyer noted flatly that he really didn't know the Northern State players, "and for all I know, you guys suck. And for all you know, I suck as a coach. So we'll see how this turns out."

Meyer would give Smiley and his teammate three rules, as he had given all his players for years:

Rule No. 1: Everybody takes notes.
Rule No. 2: Everybody says, "Yes, sir," "Yes, ma'am," "No,
sir," and "No, ma'am." In other words, be courteous to
everybody.
Rule No. 3: Everybody picks up trash.

Smiley walked out of the room confused. Meyer came to Northern State as a renowned and revered coach, with more than a quarter-century of coaching. The two highest scorers in college basketball history, John Pierce and Philip Hutcheson, had played for Meyer. But in that first meeting, he had seemed so odd.

In time, Smiley would understand.

Meyer had given players those three rules for decades. Meyer talked about technical adjustments to an offense or defense, or strategic points of emphasis. But so much of what he discussed, and what the players wrote down, was about personal accountability, about being unselfish, about serving others. When Meyer felt particularly inspired by a story or wise advice from someone, his players noticed that he would get goose bumps on his arms and on his neck.

Players like Richard Taylor would take down his words daily throughout the year, every year; Taylor usually jotted a full page of notes every day, listening for the central truth in what Meyer talked about, rather than attempting to take down every word. It was as if Meyer were speaking about two parallel universes—a player's existence on the team, and the player's existence in life.

Sept. 20, 1985
Rules on Winning
1. Work hard.
2. Stick together.
3. Have the right attitude.
4. Be positive; don't criticize, look to compliment.
5. Improve every day, especially as a person.
6. "How badly do I want it?"
7. Know that no one can beat you; you beat yourself. Morale is what motivates the best to get better. As you think, so you shall be. A spirit of devotion and enthusiasm for the team and purpose . . . Until you find a purpose higher than winning, you will never win.

Dean Smith [says]: "The single most important factor is team morale."

Nov. 3, 1985
No trash on the floor in the locker room.

Winning is a by-product of hard work—but winning is not the most important thing. Playing the game the right way is the important thing.

Nov. 30, 1985
Be sure that you are happy playing basketball. Enjoy the things that make us better—intangibles. Don't worry about stats. Worry about team concept.
"What can I do to make the team better?"
Don't be too proud to do dirty jobs.

Jan. 16, 1986
Belief—Faith—Only think success.
We want to improve every day.
You have next-game mentality when you win or lose.
We have to get everything out of everybody.
We practice and play with the intensity and poise of a national championship team.
All that is worthwhile in life is [done through] improvement.

Feb. 15, 1986
Play each possession like it's the last game.
The purpose of playing is to make your team better.
If you think about losing, you will lose.
We are the standard by which this league is measured.
Don't look ahead—don't look back—concentrate on the present task.

On March 18, 1986, David Lipscomb won the NAIA's national championship, in Kansas City, Missouri. After the game, Taylor wrote this in his notebook during the team meeting:

Thankful
Unselfish
Team—teammates
Remember this team, friends.
What would my feelings be if we lost?
There's more worth in the struggle than the championship.

The team's next meeting was a week later, from which Taylor wrote two sentences:

ACADEMICS—No excuse for bad grades—earn your grades.
Failure stays with those who stay with some success made
yesterday.

In the years after he graduated, Taylor kept all of his notebooks in a bookcase behind his desk at work, and from time to time, he would pull them out and look through them and discover words that fit a challenge he happened to cope with that day. He was convinced that the best academic experience he had at David Lipscomb—the best preparation for his personal and professional future—was playing basketball under Meyer.

The undercurrent in Meyer's message was distinctly American. The pursuit of excellence was inalienable, and excellence could be yours if you worked hard enough, if you did the right things the right way. And in fact, if you worked hard, you deserved excellence. He pounded this philosophy into his players, making them feel they had control over the rest of their lives.

Through experience and time, the players also came to understand and appreciate Meyer's personality. A reason he probably wasn't comfortable in those one-on-one conversations was that he really didn't talk about himself much; he lived out his mantras about being unselfish to the point where he thought it better to focus on anything besides himself. He had a self-deprecating sense of humor and could laugh at jokes about his baldness, his shape, his notorious frugality.

To say that Coach was cheap, one of his former players said later, would be like saying that the sun is warm. John Pierce, a center for Meyer at David Lipscomb, recalled riding in Meyer's car with him on a busy road, when suddenly the coach pulled off and stopped and got out—to pick up an empty can. He did this routinely, and as Pierce explained, you could say that he was being a good citizen, a one-man army fighting on behalf of the environment, but the truth was that to Meyer, the can was worth a nickel.

His humor would come through, sometimes unintentionally. During a practice at David Lipscomb in the nineties, Meyer barreled into a rage over repeated mistakes, and he ordered the players to just start running. A ball bounced in front of Meyer, and he slammed it straight down at the floor with both hands, but it came up so hard that it hit Meyer in the chin. The players saw this out of the corners of their eyes and their chests filled with laughter that they didn't dare let escape—and knowing this, Meyer got even more angry, taking the basketball and taking a long stride to punt it. And he fell right on his backside.

By now, the players were all but gagging on their laughter, and yet, nobody said a word. At the end of practice, the players came together for their usual end-of-practice huddle, to stack their hands up together. That's when Andy Blackston, a senior, had to say something. "Hey, Coach," Blackston said, "I hear the

Chicago Bears are looking for a new punter." Meyer raced off the floor, snapping over his shoulder, "Yeah, Blackston, well, I might be looking for a new point guard."

Once he was out of sight of the players, and alone with his assistant coaches, Meyer burst out laughing. When Meyer made a videotape years later about his coaching, he made the punting episode a centerpiece.

The players came to realize that Meyer wanted them to hold themselves accountable in the way that he did: To make the team better. To make them better.

The players noticed that after they agreed to play for Meyer in college, his handling of them would change dramatically. When they were kids attending his summer camps, he was demanding but wouldn't criticize their play directly. But the instant that they signed scholarship offers, everything changed. Richard Taylor had been in Meyer's camps for four years in high school, and when Taylor signed with David Lipscomb College, Meyer pulled him aside. "You have to totally destroy your body," Meyer advised him, "and totally rebuild it." Translated: Taylor needed to greatly improve his speed and quickness.

Meyer did not believe in showering his players with compliments or encouragement; if he did not criticize their technique, their execution, this was to be taken as a sign that they hadn't screwed up. Meyer believed he had to get his players to divorce themselves emotionally from outside factors like the score or the crowd, to push themselves beyond exhaustion or pain, and above all to instinctively set aside the concerns for their own play and do the right thing for the team. Meyer knew that the more the players feared him and reacted to him, the less they would be susceptible to those intangibles that tended to distract players. Not only would his voice be the loudest in the gym where Meyer's team was playing, it would be the *only* voice that his players heard. In a sense, he wanted to be the toughest obstacle they would deal with; anything else would be easier for them. The crowd at Belmont College? No big deal. Referees who might've missed a call? A secondary concern when Meyer was yelling at you to get better position.

Meyer coached that their goal should be small and immediate: Execute the next play properly. That's all.

When you had the ball on offense, you focused on making the right decisions in that moment and executing correctly, with the proper mechanics. Each time the team was on defense, the challenge was the same. This is why Meyer stopped and started practices constantly, to loudly note that players had approached the trap the wrong way, or that there was a moment when the ball could've—and should've—gone into the post, or that the offensive player who had position in the post had not demanded the ball effectively.

Meyer did not place emphasis on the whole, on the final score; he wanted his players to do each small thing with excellence—knowing that if they did that successfully, if they properly focused on the process and not the product, then the end result would be great. As his players progressed through the program and graduated, many came to see this as perfect training for the lives ahead of them, which played out day by day, in small elements. If they could focus on those moments, they believed they would accomplish great things: with their families, with their friendships, with their work. "Do the next right thing right," he had told them, time and again.

Meyer was direct and blunt and intense, a cauldron that could boil over during practices or games. Once, his team at David Lipscomb played a terrible first half in their home gym. Halftimes at home for Lipscomb were spent in the team room, with the players sitting at desks, their notebooks open. Their mistakes in the first half of that game were so egregious that as

Meyer sputtered, spit flew out and landed on the notebook pages of those sitting in the front row. Meyer angrily ordered them to put their notebooks away, and the players obeyed for fear that Meyer might boot them in the rear as they left the room.

David Lipscomb was a college affiliated with the Church of Christ. After a particularly grueling workout, one player griped, "This isn't what Jesus Christ would do—he would help players."

Meyer insisted that they work to help one another. He instituted a buddy system for the players, so that each one of them was responsible for two other players before each workout and practice session. They had to be in contact with their roommate and one other player who lived in another room. Wade Tomlinson's assigned buddy, besides his roommate, was Paul Sharp, who happened to be the only married player on the David Lipscomb team. Tomlinson dutifully made his call at five thirty every morning, as required, cringing when he would hear Sharp's wife groggily answer the phone. He was just following orders.

Meyer's summer camps were long days for the counselors, but Meyer was usually a little more relaxed, because the players could be the coaches, rather than coached themselves. At the end of the day, the counselors would go through some drills while the young campers rested and watched. Once Steve Smiley, who had played for three years under Meyer, was sloppy through some of the half-hour workout. When it was over, Meyer berated Smiley in front of the campers. "Steve, I think you're too satisfied," he snapped. "You're coasting, your workout was garbage, and you better start getting after it! I don't want satisfied players." Smiley was embarrassed—he had been called out in front of young teenagers, after all—and a little angry. In time, he recognized that what Meyer was trying to accomplish, beyond addressing an ugly practice, was to take advantage of an opportunity to push a player whose leadership would be needed in his senior season.

The players would come to understand the reasons for

Meyer's approach, but this didn't make it any easier when they were in the midst of the harsh treatment. During the 1985–86 season at David Lipscomb, Meyer was furious about the way the Bisons had executed in practice—somebody had made a selfish decision, which Meyer saw as a symptom of a larger problem that this team was having—and so one day he told his players to start running. For the next seventy-five minutes, they went up and back, end line to end line for a while, and then did what was called the Fire Drill, and then Suicides, Meyer hectoring them the whole way.

As the last sprint was completed, Bob Ford, one of the team's leaders, veered off into the team's locker room without saying a word. When the other players reached the locker room, they saw that Ford had cleaned out his stuff—and by the time some of them rushed back to his dorm room, Ford had emptied that, too, and was in a car on his way home. Ford decided to come back a couple of days later, and for years, players on that team were convinced that this practice had been a turning point in their season. Thereafter, Taylor thought, players set aside their own agendas completely and focused on what was needed in each possession. The Bisons finished the season 35–4, winning five games at the NAIA national championship tournament in Kansas City.

Three years later, David Lipscomb was ranked number one in the country near the end of the regular season, with a 38–1 record, and the Bisons suffered a heartbreaking season-ending loss in their own gym to Belmont. It was the kind of stunning defeat that can wreck the composure of a coach or players, and afterward, Meyer had met with the players, who all had their notebooks open. Jason Shelton wrote down what he said:

Coach is proud of us as a team.
Remember the seniors.

Have a spirit of resolve to improve.
Don't whip yourself to death about this loss; only one team wins
*   the last game of their season.*
The measurement of a man is his response to adversity.

Make every place better than it was before you arrived, Meyer had told the players, and specifically, he insisted that they apply this when they traveled as a team. Rick Byrd, the coach at Belmont, recalled that after the first home game he had coached against Lipscomb, the visiting gym—where the Bisons players dressed—was left spotless, with the used towels neatly arranged. On top of the pile, there was a piece of paper: a thank-you note from John Kimbrell, the team's center and best player. Byrd would coach against Meyer's teams for years, a rivalry of two schools located two miles apart on the same street, both contenders for NAIA championships, and no matter what Byrd thought about the aptitude of a particular team, he knew that the kids who came out of the Lipscomb program were good kids.

Meyer had pounded into their brains, in practice and in the players' classroom work, the concept of not compounding mistakes, of training themselves to think rationally in moments of stress, rather than rushing or panicking. NBA, he called it: Next Best Action. See the need, fill the need, he had told them, over and over.

Meyer sponged these kinds of thoughts and mantras from books, from articles, from people he knew. After moving to Aberdeen, he befriended a preacher named Dick Ward, and as Ward talked, Meyer would pull out his notebook, jot down his thoughts, and pass them on to his players. Ward—who had traveled extensively in the world and had known great tragedy in his life—told Meyer what to remember when you are in a crisis:

Keep alert. Stay calm. Do not be afraid.

Kyle Schwan played four years for Meyer at Northern State and came to think of him as the toughest person he knew. He had never seen Meyer in a fistfight, and in the years that he knew him, Meyer had gained a little weight and gotten soft around the middle. But his toughness, as Schwan saw it, was Meyer's emotional relentlessness, the way that he attacked every day and every situation with the same demand for excellence. His drive seemed unbreakable.

And when Schwan went to talk to Dick Ward—the preacher who had provided Meyer with that mantra *Keep alert. Stay calm. Do not be afraid*—he mentioned to Ward that in the first seconds after Meyer's head-on collision with the semi on Highway 20, when Schwan was running down the road and still didn't know what had happened, he expected his coach to angrily climb out of his car and kick the crap out of the truck driver.

But seeing the crumpled car and Meyer pressed limply against the seat, Schwan wasn't sure if Meyer was still alive.

CHAPTER 3

Matt Hammer could see Don Meyer's wrecked car in the distance, but he didn't know what to expect when he reached his coach. Debris was scattered all over the road; there was no smoke or fire coming from the car. By the time Hammer got there, two of Northern State's players, Brett Newton and Kyle Schwan, were already at the driver's-side door.

Meyer was dazed, his breathing heavy, the deployed air bag deflated in front of him. Blood dripped down the bridge of his nose. Glass from the shattered windows was everywhere inside the car. Suddenly, Hammer saw Meyer's eyes focus, as if he had awakened. "Is everyone okay?" Meyer asked softly.

By now, all of Northern State's players had gathered around

the car, and Schwan and Kevin Ratzsch, the team's seniors, immediately ordered the youngest players to stand to the side of the vehicle, about twenty feet away, and form a prayer circle. A couple of older players went onto the road to direct traffic. Tom Giesen, a sophomore, was already on the road, trying to call 911—but on this remote road, there was no signal.

Giesen ran to the crest of the road and tried again; still, no signal. He kept moving frantically up the highway, toward the highest ground he could find, dialing a third time—and this time, he reached the Faulk County Sheriff's Office at Faulkton, South Dakota, a town of eight hundred. It was 4:51 P.M.

Sheriff Kurt Hall had been on the road for much of the day delivering civil papers—a summons or two. When the 911 came in, Hall and two deputies immediately jumped into a car, with Hall at the wheel. The greatest risk for those injured in South Dakota car accidents is often lethal bleeding, because of the long distances that emergency personnel must travel. The state trooper on patrol that day, Carl Stearns, was responsible for covering an area that ranged two hundred miles from north to south.

What Hall had told his own deputies about driving to an emergency situation was this: Use your lights and sirens, and drive as fast as you can within the limitations created by the conditions. This was a beautiful fall afternoon, and the distance to the site was twenty-one miles. Hall raced along the two-lane roads.

At Meyer's car, Hammer pulled out his phone and called Randy Baruth, Meyer's assistant coach, who had left Aberdeen about ten minutes after the Northern State caravan. Hammer sounded out of breath. "Coach had a flat tire or something and he's been hit by a semi," Hammer said.

Baruth was annoyed. "Matt, that's really not very funny," he said.

"No," Hammer said. "Coach has been hit by a semi and it doesn't look good."

Baruth mashed his gas pedal to the floor.

Hammer climbed into the passenger side of Meyer's vehicle, and Schwan and Newton stood at the window on the driver's side and talked to Meyer. They could not tell that every rib in the left side of his chest was broken. His diaphragm—the muscle that lines the rib cage—had been torn away from the bone and his spleen had been irreparably damaged. His liver was lacerated. His left wrist started to swell and it looked as if his wristwatch was going to pop off. The players gently wiped shattered glass away from his face.

"I'm sorry," Meyer said, repeatedly. He tried leaning forward in his seat, bobbing forward against the seat belt, but the players told him to lean back and stay still. Newton held the belt away from Meyer's chest, and Hammer, Newton, and Schwan got him to focus on taking steady, measured breaths. The players would later be haunted by the tortured sound.

Meyer mentioned that his left leg was hurt, but with the driver's panel crushed backward against the seat, the players couldn't really see his leg. They could see that he was struggling for consciousness, and worked to keep him awake.

Newton and Schwan led Meyer in a recital of the Lord's Prayer, and the group of younger players nearby spoke the same words:

Our Father, which art in heaven, Hallowed be Thy Name, Thy kingdom come, Thy will be done . . .

The wait for help began. The players already felt as if hours had passed.

A few hours earlier, Dr. Michael Snyder had attended the funeral of an aunt in Pierre, South Dakota, and he had intended to drive on Highway 212 on his way back to Marshall, Minnesota, where he lived and worked as a surgeon. But construction caused him to bypass 212 altogether and turn onto Highway 20, a nice little two-lane road.

After just a few miles on Highway 20, he saw cars all over the side of the road. An accident. Already someone was out on the road stopping traffic—a woman, he recalled, who was insistent that nobody should try to pass; she had no intention of letting Snyder go by. But Snyder told her that he was a doctor, and she let him through.

There was no emergency help yet on the scene, and Snyder stopped near Meyer's car and went to the driver's-side window and identified himself to everyone. What he saw was encouraging: Meyer was talking and alert. If he wasn't speaking, or if he was incomprehensible, then there was a chance that the steering wheel had smashed back into his chest and damaged his aorta to the point that blood was being cut off from his brain. That Meyer was talking at all was a good sign.

Snyder chatted with Meyer about his background, about how he was a South Dakota native who had grown up in Pierre, and as he did so, he ducked his head into the window and looked down toward the floorboard. Meyer's left leg was shattered, pointing at nearly a right angle toward the passenger seat. Blood seeped through his pant leg, onto the floor of the car.

Meyer mentioned that his leg was hurt, but Snyder thought it best not to focus on that. He told Meyer that he could get him out, if need be, but it would be better for emergency personnel to extricate him from the car. It was still unclear if Meyer might have spinal cord damage, and so long as he was conscious and talking, Snyder felt that it was best to wait.

Standing next to Schwan and Newton, and seeing the prayer circle of the youngest Northern State players, Snyder was immediately struck by how composed the players were.

Meyer started talking about how he felt tired. "I've got to go to sleep," he said to them. That's when Schwan started yelling at his coach in the way that Meyer had long yelled at him. "Narrow focus!" Schwan said, parroting words that Meyer had aimed at him. There was a telephone pole nearby and Schwan told Meyer to concentrate on the telephone pole.

In the drawer of his desk at Northern State, Meyer kept a bag of walnuts as a symbol of toughness, handing them out to the players. Schwan drew on this: "You're a tough nut! C'mon! Remember the nuts—we're tough nuts! Narrow focus!"

Baruth arrived, pulled up his car, and went over to the side of the car. "I'm going to be all right," Meyer told him. "You take the players on the retreat."

Baruth wasn't thinking about that. He and the others on the scene kept waiting for help to arrive. There was none in sight yet.

Meyer stayed awake, but his breathing was becoming more shallow. Schwan saw tiny particles of glass on Meyer's lips, and he began to think about the possibility that he or Newton or somebody would have to administer CPR, and how he would get the glass off Meyer's mouth. That's when they heard the approaching sirens.

Sheriff Kurt Hall had covered the twenty-one miles in fourteen minutes, and as his cruiser reached the accident site at 5:05 Hall saw a group of young men huddled near a smashed vehicle on the side of the road. *Great—some college kids trying to get a look at some blood,* he thought with exasperation.

But as Hall came out of his vehicle and told the young men to move to the side, they complied, all of them calm and composed. He ascertained that they were basketball team members, and that the injured man in the car was their coach. Dr. Snyder went to Sheriff Hall and told him that they would need a helicopter as soon as possible. He was concerned about the blood loss. Surgeons refer to the first hour after an accident as the Golden

Hour, and unless Meyer was moved quickly, he would be at greater risk.

Trintje Bauer, part of Faulkton's volunteer ambulance service, arrived right after Hall, having raced to the site with her husband, and the information she had been told by the time she arrived was sketchy. The Northern State basketball team had been involved in an accident, a head-on situation with a semi. The possibility that a van full of players had been smashed by the semi lodged in her mind, and as she and her husband pulled up to the accident scene, she saw cars all over the place. She went right to Meyer's car, where Baruth was standing.

"Who else is hurt?" she asked.

"That's it," Baruth said.

"You're kidding me," Bauer blurted out. All of these vehicles, all of these young men, she thought, the truck driver . . . and nobody other than Meyer was hurt. A miracle.

But as the players stepped away from the car and Bauer climbed into the passenger seat of Meyer's car, she could see how serious the injuries were. A hospital helicopter was called from Aberdeen, thirty-six miles away. Bauer attached an IV bag to Meyer, who was still conscious. "I'm sorry," he said. "I think I messed up."

Bauer reassured Meyer, kept talking to him, in an effort to keep him conscious. Meyer kept talking about his players, apologizing. "Those poor boys don't need to see this," Meyer said.

Bauer could hear his breathing getting shallower; he was losing ground, she thought. Meyer started to slip in and out of consciousness, and about that time the helicopter landed—at 5:27, thirty-six minutes after the 911 call. Firemen popped open Meyer's car with the hydraulic Jaws of Life, Meyer was lifted out, and it was then that his left leg became visible. The lower half, from just below the knee, was in the shape of the letter *V,* folded backward, with the bone sticking out through the torn pant leg. His left sock was saturated with blood.

Within fifteen minutes after landing, the helicopter lifted off Highway 20. Bauer, the paramedic, turned to check on the players again. Sometimes, after the adrenaline wears off in the aftermath of an accident, injuries become apparent.

Don Carda, the driver of the truck, was unhurt, and he stood to the side, badly shaken. Schwan walked over to him and hugged him. "There was nothing you could have done," Schwan said to Carda. "It wasn't your fault." Carda moved to the side and leaned against a car, and another player, Mitch Boeck, stayed with him.

Some players began to weep. "Is he going to lose his leg?" one of them asked her.

"Is he going to die?" another asked.

Bauer tried reassuring them. The truth was she didn't know.

Baruth turned on the hazard lights on his car and he and Hammer raced back to Aberdeen at close to 100 mph, to get to the hospital. "How bad do you think his left leg is hurt?" Hammer asked Baruth.

"I don't know anything about surgery," Baruth replied, "but I don't know how they can save anything that looks like that."

At about the same time that the sheriff arrived on the accident site, Jackie Witlock—the associate director of athletic development at Northern State and a friend of the Meyers'—got a call about Meyer's accident, and was asked to contact Carmen Meyer.

Carmen was at a high school football game in Aberdeen, and Witlock drove to the parking lot and called her from there. "There's been a little accident," Witlock told her.

"Oh, I'm going to kill him," Carmen Meyer said. She and Don had been married for forty-one years, and she had long worried that her husband's voracious work habits, stubbornness, and exhaustion would cause him to fall asleep at the wheel. "Is it bad?" Carmen Meyer asked. "Did he fall asleep?"

Witlock didn't have a lot of details. She had been told only that a semi had blown a tire and hit Meyer's car. They went to St. Luke's and waited, and as the time passed, concern about the unknown grew. The helicopter landed, Meyer was unloaded and rolled past Carmen, and she saw the smock of the EMT at the head of the gurney near Meyer's head perfectly red in color. It was covered with blood.

The doctors in Aberdeen saw the condition of Meyer's leg and made the decision to move him to the hospital in Sioux Falls immediately. A friend, John Schwan, father of Kyle Schwan, offered Carmen Meyer the use of his private plane to fly to Sioux Falls, and Carmen returned to her house to collect some things.

A state trooper called Carmen and told her to return to the hospital immediately, and she and Baruth headed back to the hospital. "Why would they want me to come back?" Carmen said, and Baruth tried to think of anything other than the obvious: that Meyer was near death, and they wanted Carmen back at the hospital for the end of his life.

Baruth pulled up at the curb of the hospital and Carmen rushed in, passing a state trooper, who looked at Baruth. His face was sheet-white, and he shook his head slightly. Carmen saw the faces of the doctors and thought that they were thinking this would be the last time she would see him alive.

But Meyer clung to life.

On the forty-five-minute flight to Sioux Falls, Carmen Meyer prayed and said little. Baruth tried encouraging her. "He's tough, he's going to make it," he said. Baruth instinctively began writing a to-do list—of who needed to be contacted, what needed to be done for the basketball players, how the team's schedule would be affected—trying to keep his mind occupied.

The plane got to Sioux Falls before the helicopter that carried Meyer, and at Avera McKennan Hospital, there was a short wait before Meyer was taken into surgery. By then, Meyer was attached to tubes and wires; Carmen Meyer and Baruth spoke to him briefly before he was wheeled away.

The trauma surgeon on duty that night, Dr. David Strand, had gotten advance notice that a victim from a head-on car accident was being flown from Aberdeen, a male with a leg and possible head injury. The operating room, the lab, and others were alerted.

When Strand first saw Meyer, Meyer was awake and alert. But he was pale, with his blood pressure elevated. It was clear immediately to Strand that there was blood collecting in Meyer's abdomen, and while Meyer's left leg was in awful condition, the priority was his internal injuries.

Strand made a long abdominal incision; blood poured out, and he went about trying to control the bleeding. As he looked around Meyer's organs to find the sources of bleeding, stapling them as he went, he saw something that made his heart sink.

The mesentery, the tissue that connects the small intestine to the abdominal wall, was withdrawn, puckered—like a divot on a golf course—and there, in the small intestine, were tumors that Strand knew, with near certainty, were cancerous. There were tumors in Meyer's liver as well.

Strand figured that there was a good chance the Meyers weren't aware of the cancer. Sometime that night, he would have to update the wife of the man on the table about not only his life-threatening injuries, he would have to tell her, *There's something else: Your husband has cancer, and he will probably die from that.* Your job is to help people, Strand felt, and then you find something like this.

In a waiting room right outside where Strand was operating, Carmen Meyer sat on a chair, Witlock on a couch; Baruth sat on

Don Meyer's car on September 5, 2008.

the floor. At about three A.M., Strand emerged from the operating room, pulled up a seat next to where Carmen was sitting, and walked her through the work he had done.

"We've been working really hard on him," he said. "We've had to stop several times to get his blood pressure right, and there were a few times that it was touch and go."

A chest tube had to be inserted because of all the blood loss, Strand explained. There were lacerations on the liver. There was damage to a lung. A lot of work had been done in his chest cavity. "The spleen couldn't be saved," Strand said. "We had to remove some of his small intestines."

Strand mentioned that the surgical team hadn't started addressing Meyer's leg, given the priorities.

"I need to ask you something," Strand said. "Did you know that your husband has cancer?"

CHAPTER 4

Carmen McCune was a freshman at Northern Colorado University in February of 1967, working part-time in the equipment room at the athletic department. She mentioned to a friend that she had noticed a handsome junior who played basketball and baseball named Don Meyer. Not long after that, Meyer approached the window of the equipment room. He looked at the ceiling, and without preamble asked if she would like to go out after the basketball game that night.

"Well, sure, that would be great," she said. Without saying anything more, he walked away, neglecting to set a time or a place for their date.

Carmen McCune assumed that she was to wait for him after

the game. It turned out that Meyer's parents attended the game as well, and Meyer's mother, Edna, had heard from another student—not her son, of course—that the freshman co-ed standing outside the locker room was to be her son's date for the evening of February 18, 1967. Edna Meyer proceeded to ask Carmen about how Don had been doing in school and about how he had been eating, because Don did not provide that type of information.

Carmen McCune had no answers. "I don't know," she said awkwardly. Because she hadn't actually exchanged any words with the young man other than to say yes to this date, she knew nothing about him.

She would learn in the days ahead that Donald Wayne Meyer had been born on December 16, 1944, the first child of Don and Edna Meyer, a wartime yield of a 404-acre farm in Wayne, Nebraska. His father, a marine, was in the service when he was born. The boy was expected to do what his grandfather and his father and mother had done: work hard across the rolling hills of their farm. Without complaint. Without questions. The Meyers had a couple of hundred beef cattle—some Angus, some Herefords— and dairy cows and pigs. They grew oats and some soybeans, and spent many hours grinding corn. They fixed everything with baling wire, as farmers learn to do. The boy drove a tractor before his tenth birthday. They had running water, Don Meyer would joke years later, whenever anyone carrying the water buckets ran to the house; otherwise, the Meyers had walking water, with an outhouse.

His grandfather Carl F. Meyer was known to the neighbors as Carl F., and he wore that middle initial with pride. There was a picture taken of Carl F. wearing a jungle hat with a wide brim, his hands on his overall straps—the proud pose of a farmer.

His oldest grandson was scared of Carl F. Years later, Don

Meyer could still hear the ominous sound of his grandfather's truck pulling into the driveway and the family dogs barking; he could still remember his siblings hiding. Carl F. took care of the family haircuts with clippers out by the woodshed.

And the eldest son was intimidated by his father, who believed in discipline as much as he believed in hard labor. Once, the pigs escaped their pen and the boy was charged with the responsibility of recapturing them. When he couldn't do it, his father kicked him, over and over. Years later, the son would tell the story with gallows humor, mentioning that his father could've been a punter in the National Football League. The father's logic was that since his son was smarter than the pigs, he should have found a way to contain them.

The father didn't really teach his children about how to fix machinery; he expected that they would just learn how through observation. One day, Don was on the tractor, sowing oats, and a strange pinging sound started coming from the engine. The boy didn't know what it was, and kept driving. Shortly thereafter the engine seized; the tractor had run out of oil. This also earned him a butt-kicking. As did the time when he planted the oats in misaligned rows, which became clear when the plants grew during the summer.

There had been no instructions, no guidance, and after the son became a coach, he thought of his father and how his style might fit in among coaches. He decided that his father wouldn't have been a good teacher but would have been an excellent motivator. The Meyer children learned about work ethic and about discipline; no other way was acceptable.

The son also played sports, and he loved baseball—and loved playing it, pitching for local teams. For the rest of his life, he could recite in the manner of an oral historian specific details from the games in which he had played or seen and heard. Like the time when he pitched a game with sunburned shoulders, at age ten. Like listening to Harry Caray broadcasts of Cardinals games on KMOX, on the radio in his room, with the windows open and the summer breeze coming through. Like when his uncle had served as the catcher for another Nebraskan, Bob Gibson, and came away with his hand feeling like raw meat. Like the time when his father told him it was his choice whether to pitch with a tired arm, and the boy had looked over and saw a man with no legs sitting in a wheelchair, and figured that he could pitch a baseball game and be okay.

But while the father liked baseball and approved of his son playing sports, the games would never supersede the work to be done on the farm. Once a baseball tryout was scheduled at a nearby town, a prearranged opportunity for the son. That day's job on the farm—getting hay into the barn before rain fell—wasn't finished in time. And the father looked at the son and said flatly, "You're not going anywhere. This has got to get done." That was that. Don Meyer was sure his father would have preferred that he had gotten the chance to play, but work was work and the lines between work and all else were immovable.

The son hustled home from school to watch the World Series, when games came on their black-and-white television. He was nine years old in the summer of 1954 and had closely followed the Cleveland Indians, a team that was loaded with pitching and had won 111 games in the regular season. They faced the New York Giants in the World Series, and watching those games was the first time the boy could recall having a sense of life beyond the boundaries of his family's farm.

The son loved reading, school, and sports. He really didn't like farming and didn't have a knack for it, which made it even more difficult to achieve what meant so much to him: the affirmation of his father. There would be none to his face; his father didn't believe in that. There were no hugs; emotions were not expressed out loud. The boy's bedroom was located just over his parents' bedroom, and sometimes the son would slowly, carefully roll open the heat grate and hope to hear his father to say something positive about him to his mother. He felt his father loved him, but never heard the words.

On the day that Meyer left for college, he went to say goodbye. He walked into the barn, where his father was doing the milking, squatting down between cows. "I'm leaving," the son said.

The father didn't move, didn't stand up, didn't step out from between the cows. "Well, work hard and don't get into trouble," the father said.

Don Meyer came back to work on the farm the summer after his freshman year, and one day when working outside the barn, a preacher drove into the yard with horrible news. Jerry Meyer, his younger brother, had drowned. He'd been in an irrigation ditch and the undertow had pulled him under the surface. The father told his eldest son to go get the truck and gave him a verbal list of all those to whom he needed to take the news about Jerry. The son thought he would get through the service without breaking down, but when he saw his little brother in the casket, his emotions overcame him.

He went back to Northern Colorado at the end of the summer, with a farmer's ethics built into him in the way a bearing wall is part of a house. He took with him three small pieces of machinery from the farm—a bolt from a windrower, a grease bucket from a corn grinder, and a cotter key from a windmill. But through his college years, he would leave the farm behind and begin a family of his own.

Carmen McCune had been drawn to him partly because he was a good athlete and handsome, and partly because he had no pretensions. He wasn't some smooth operator. He was just himself, and she appreciated that. They were both competitive, too. She played softball, and he took her out and hit ground balls at her, very hard. "Stay down on the ball," he'd say. She had grown up playing cards and board games and he had not, and after she finally talked him into playing checkers, Carmen quickly took control of the game. Aware that he was going to lose, he flipped the board over with a laugh, the checkers flying everywhere. They never played again.

The first time that Don Meyer went to her home, driving in a borrowed car, he saw her brother J.D. playing a game with cards. Meyer sat down and tried to follow along as J.D. played what seemed like some kind of solitaire game; he would hold the deck of cards, and he'd turn them over, one by one, and look at them, and Don Meyer tried to follow the game, throwing down cards in the same way that J.D. did. This was the first time that Don Meyer, from a small town, had ever been around anyone with Down's syndrome. J.D. had no rules for his game; he simply enjoyed playing with the cards. In retrospect, Meyer said, laughing, maybe the McCunes thought Meyer was the dumbest person they had ever seen.

J.D., four years younger than Carmen, loved people and loved hugs, and J.D. and Meyer liked each other right away, something that greatly impressed Carmen in these first days of dating. And Meyer was drawn to the McCunes: Bob and Mae McCune were outgoing and funny and warm, and they treated Don like a son immediately. Bob McCune would make it a point to go see Meyer pitch for Northern Colorado, and Meyer went to church with the McCunes. It was then that he learned to study the Bible. Years later, Meyer thought that there were two different types of parenting, and he thought he had benefited from both.

About three months after their first date, Don and Carmen

took a walk together in Glenmere Park, and he said, "I would like for us to get married. I would like it to be in August." He hoped that he would be selected in Major League Baseball's June amateur draft, he explained, and if that happened, the wedding would have to be postponed. "Well, okay," she said, and Carmen was torn on the eve of the draft, because on one hand, she knew that her fiancé wanted to play baseball, but she also very much wanted to be married. He was not drafted—this broke his heart—but six months and a day after that first date, twenty-two-year-old Don Meyer and nineteen-year-old Carmen McCune married. He bought her a ring for ninety dollars, she sold her clarinet for seventy dollars to pay for her wedding dress, and they married at the Church of Christ in Greeley, Colorado. (On their twenty-fifth wedding anniversary, Don purchased another ring for Carmen.)

The Meyers' first child, Jeremy James—his first name chosen in memory of Don Meyer's younger brother, and his middle name picked in honor of Carmen's brother—was born in 1969, and Brooke and Brittney followed in the next three years. He made a living as a coach, and she made the trains run on time in the Meyer home. In one of his first summers after he became the head coach at Hamline University, in St. Paul, he worked camps away from his wife and children, and over a six-week period, he was home for four hours, leaving Carmen Meyer to raise the children.

The Meyer children realized that their mother directed the ship; she made sure to get them to their team events and was primarily responsible for doling out the discipline. If Don Meyer's team lost a game, Carmen tended to be even more angry than he was after the defeat, seething about some late-game mistake or missed free throw; her kids would tell stories years later about the morose car rides back home, which they thought said a lot about how competitive their mother was. If there was any kind of con-

Don and Carmen Meyer on their wedding day.

test played between Carmen and the children, she had fun, but they knew she was in it to win, whether it was a board game or counting license plates or road signs on the two-day summer drives to see grandparents out west.

Carmen fixed everything around the house—as Don Meyer's father would have expected—and Don coached. Once, Carmen asked him to help put a crib together, and after fussing with it for a while, he tossed the tool aside and said, "This is just too tedious. I can't do it."

As soon as the youngest child, Brittney, started school—after the family had moved to Nashville—Carmen Meyer enrolled at Lipscomb and earned her undergraduate degree and went to Tennessee State to get her master's. The Meyer children would think of their parents as equally driven. The summer basketball camps at Lipscomb—the largest in the country—were a Meyer family production. Don Meyer coached, and Carmen ran the concessions, with help from the kids as they got older. They would remain in Nashville for twenty-four years, their children growing into adults in that time.

Meyer quit his job at David Lipscomb University in Nashville in the spring of 1999, after a disagreement on principle with the administration. He tried pursuing the job at Vanderbilt University, but felt that the higher-profile school would prefer a Division I coach rather than a small-college coach from the same city. He tried and failed to get the job at Pepperdine.

But Meyer never really threw himself into the pursuit of a Division I job. His love of basketball was in the coaching, the teaching, and at the Division I level, the potential for complications was enormous. Meyer had heard the horror stories about the cheating that went on at some schools at the Division I level, about the influence and infiltration of school boosters and administration, the disproportionate (in his eyes) focus on wins and losses. He wanted to teach young men what he thought was the right way, and, generally speaking, he wanted his program to be left alone.

After he quit at Lipscomb, however, he had no program. He had no job. Some coaches with his résumé might have decided to wait for a perfect opportunity to open up, and might have sat out a year. But Meyer had never trusted inactivity; it made him anxious. He trusted work. The hardest time of every season for him had always been right after the end of a basketball season, when the program went dormant and there wasn't a lot of recruiting to do; he tended to get depressed.

At about the same time that Meyer left his job at Lipscomb, Bob Olson, the basketball coach at Northern State, in Aberdeen, South Dakota, had agreed to become athletic director. Initially, it was unclear whether Olson would coach the 1999–2000 season. He decided to look for a replacement, and if he couldn't find someone suitable, he would just coach the basketball team himself. Don Meyer heard about the job opening and reached out to Olson, who knew Meyer but was still curious as to why such an accomplished coach would be interested in the Northern State job.

However, Meyer was very interested. He told Olson that he wanted the team, that he wanted to be able to coach in a place where he could run the program the way he wanted, without interference from the athletic director or people outside the university. And so it was, late in the summer of 1999, that Meyer left Nashville pulling a U-Haul trailer, to go to Aberdeen, South Dakota, as quickly as possible.

Jerry Krause, who had been a coach at Northern Colorado when Meyer played there and a friend to Meyer for almost thirty years, asked Meyer if taking the job at Northern State was really a move he wanted to make. He suggested to Meyer that maybe it would be good to wait until the following spring, when there would be more job openings. Coaching in the Dakotas, Krause knew, was a rough assignment, and he worried that many things might go wrong. But Meyer forged ahead. Carmen Meyer followed, as she always had.

When Meyer took the job at Northern State, one of the greatest concerns that Olson had was about whether Carmen would adapt to Aberdeen. She had been entrenched in Nashville, had cultivated so many strong friendships, and her grandchildren were there. Her daughters thought, half-seriously, that their mother wouldn't last a year in South Dakota.

Carmen Meyer didn't just survive in Aberdeen; she thrived. She felt liberated, in part, by the move. When they were at Lipscomb, they could not go out to a restaurant and have a glass of wine, because the school's religious doctrine was so strict. Going to South Dakota was like having a clean slate. She loved how warm the people were. The Meyers bought a house next to the golf course in the northeastern part of the town, where in the summers she would play daily. She played tennis. She bowled. She joined a Bible study group. She was in the middle of everything, it seemed. After Carmen Meyer had been in Aberdeen for almost a decade, Bob Olson wondered if she knew more people than anyone else in town.

Don Meyer focused on basketball, as he always had, building the program the way he wanted. His standing as the head coach of Northern State University placed him in the public eye. But generally speaking, he hated going to public events, feeling much more comfortable dealing with the individuals he bumped into in Aberdeen than he ever did at coat-and-tie fundraisers. His daughters had felt all along that their father did much better dealing with those who had less than those who had more; socially, he was more apt to strike up a conversation with a farmer in mud-stained boots than with a wealthy booster. This did not make it easy for Carmen Meyer on those occasions when she convinced him to go out to a charity event or dinner at a restaurant. He was apt to keep to himself, sometimes appearing rude to those who didn't know him. Jerry Meyer, the coach's son, once asked his grandmother Edna about his father's reticence, and she tried to explain it to him. "Some people just don't like to talk," Edna Meyer said.

By the summer of 2008, the silence gradually had become frustrating to Carmen. Nine years into their time in Aberdeen, they had come to live parallel lives that rarely intersected during the days. He coached basketball, and she spent time with friends and at their house; staff members at Northern State rarely saw them together. "We had gotten to the point where his tunnel vision [made it difficult]," she recalled. "He really didn't care about any of my activities, and so I sort of got hardened. We got along fine, but it was like we were leading separate lives almost."

A major source of anger for Carmen was how he repeatedly failed to alert her to the impending arrival of visiting coaches or friends. The Meyers had the basement of their home restructured to create three bedrooms, with the intention of having visitors use them. But someone would often arrive unannounced at the house, having been invited to stay for a few days by Don Meyer. Consequently, Carmen would be left to scramble to make the beds and prepare meals, without advance warning.

She had once gone down in her nightgown into the basement of what she thought was an empty house, only to see somebody's shaving kit on the counter in the bathroom. "I was always happy for people to be here," she recalled. "I just wanted him to let me know. But it just wasn't important to him if there were clean sheets on the bed, because he didn't care. He'd sleep in sheets that someone had slept in. Or he'd tell me at the last minute that he wanted to have the team over. And I'd be furious because I already had plans. Plus, he thought I could snap my fingers and have a meal ready to serve and have the house straightened up."

Randy Baruth, Meyer's assistant coach, started alerting Carmen to let her know that somebody might be coming over, or that maybe a team function would occur at her house. Then Baruth started to do some dinners at his house—to help steer the situation away from any of the tension between the Meyers, Carmen assumed. Their worst arguments had been about the lack of notice before a visitor arrived. That, and Meyer's tendency to drive when he was tired.

Don Meyer would come home in the evening and Carmen would ask him how his day had gone, and her husband would say a few words in response, or say nothing at all, not asking her in turn about her day. Eventually, Carmen Meyer found herself posing the question to him, with some internal sarcasm attached— "How was *your* day?"—because she assumed he probably wouldn't respond and probably wouldn't ask about her day. She never got much information out of him.

Now, in the first hours of September 6, 2008, it was unclear whether he would ever talk again. He was unconscious on an operating table, being worked on by a trauma surgeon. At four A.M., Carmen Meyer and Jackie Witlock started on a large one-thousand-piece jigsaw puzzle as they waited—a bright red, green, and gold puzzle of Christmas ornaments.

A couple of hours after Carmen Meyer had been told about the cancer, a nurse emerged from the operating room to retrieve Carmen; his vital signs were diminishing, and they wanted her in the room in case the worst happened. After she went in, his condition improved slightly, and Carmen returned to the waiting room. "I don't think he's going to make it," Carmen told Witlock.

"Carmen, we have to stay positive," Witlock said. "We have to keep praying."

At that very moment in Nashville, Jerry, Brooke, and Brittney were about to get on a plane to South Dakota. Carmen fretted about what she should tell them over the phone before they boarded. "Would it be like lying if I don't tell them about the cancer?" she asked Witlock. She assured Carmen it was okay, and Carmen Meyer waited—for more word of her husband's condition, for the arrival of her children.

CHAPTER 5

The first information Don Meyer's three grown children received about his accident came in fragments, through Carmen. At first they heard that the collision had not been that serious, as Carmen had initially been led to believe. The worst-case scenario was that he suffered a broken leg.

But Brooke Napier, the second of the three Meyer children, assumed all along that the news would be worse, and sure enough, word soon came from Carmen that he had been transported twice by helicopter, as his condition was assessed. He had a vascular problem, the youngest sibling, Brittney Touchton, was told, and his leg might be lost. Brooke immediately bought plane tickets for herself and Brittney and her brother, Jerry, and, unable to sleep, she prayed out loud before leaving for the airport.

Brittney, Brooke, and Jerry Meyer.

Just before the three of them got on a predawn flight out of Nashville, Brittney called Carmen once more. By then it was clear that his injuries were serious and that his life was hanging in the balance; Carmen had mentioned earlier to her daughters that his liver might be lacerated, among many other problems.

As Brittney was about to board the plane, she asked Carmen, "What about his liver?"

Carmen stumbled over her answer. "Well, the doctor didn't say much about that," she said, in such a manner that Brittney sensed there was something that Carmen didn't want to tell them.

The three siblings got on the plane, unsure of whether he would be alive when they got to Sioux Falls. Fear overwhelmed any of their efforts to read or sleep. During a layover in Minneapolis, the three of them ordered food, and Brooke found that she just couldn't eat anything. They were filled with anxiety, and had many questions and no answers.

They were the children of two driven achievers—Don Meyer, the championship-winning basketball coach, and Carmen Meyer, who seemed to be thoroughly dedicated and effective at whatever she did. Jerry was the oldest, born in 1969, and Brooke and Brittney followed within three years. They were ingrained with a desire to not disappoint either of their parents, who had set such high standards for achievement and behavior and work ethic. David Lipscomb College was affiliated with the Meyers' church, the Church of Christ, and Lipscomb operated under a strict code of conduct, as if there were additional commandments beyond the first ten.

The Meyers' lives revolved around the basketball calendar. Don Meyer did not like the time he spent away from his family, but he felt he was doing what was necessary to build a secure life for them. In order to meet his own standards for coaching effectively and successfully, he had to devote many hours to his program. There was never a moment, Brooke would say years later, when she doubted whether her father loved her, but the Meyer children shared their father with basketball; at times, they felt as if they competed with basketball. They recognized that they would have to table their own needs until after basketball was over—and for the Meyers, basketball continued almost year-round, because of the long seasons and the summer camps. In any event, their own schedules were packed.

Jerry was a baseball and basketball star, and Brooke had played basketball and softball and tennis, and she ran track. Brittney played basketball until she developed knee trouble—a God-given excuse for her not to play, she thought. She really didn't care for the sport but had always pushed ahead because so much in their lives was measured through basketball.

They played in their own games and attended the games of their siblings and their father's games; they did a lot of their homework on bleacher seats. In the summers, all the Meyers would be out the door early to run the summer camps, and they returned around midnight. During the school year, the Meyers would meet for dinner together at Captain D's on Wednesdays. On Sundays, Don Meyer and Brittney would race for the couch.

On a day-to-day basis, the Meyer children answered to Carmen. If there was a crime committed in the house, she would be the one to break down the suspect with the lecture about trust and honesty and integrity; she was the disciplinarian. Don Meyer would follow up on the punishment she had rendered by adding, "You can't do that to your mother. You have to be good for your mother." Because of the constant cycle of games and practices and recruiting trips and camps and clinics, he wasn't around a lot, and after Brooke and Brittney grew into adulthood, they agreed that it all might not have worked if he had been present all the time; Carmen and Don were both chiefs who needed elbow room.

Don was a superhero to the two daughters, someone who excelled in his high-profile position and was well respected in his community and within his program. The only time that Brittney could remember anyone saying anything bad about her father was during a basketball game against a rival, and this had upset her greatly. To his children, Don Meyer had been invulnerable and untouchable—and sometimes unreachable.

To them, he could be completely blunt or socially obtuse. Brittney could remember having meaningful conversations while driving with her father, when he would suddenly turn to her and ask, "Who do you think we should start tonight?" leaving her to wonder if he had heard her at all. Brooke had once given him a blanket for Christmas, only to be told he already had a blanket, words that had hurt her. Gift-giving, Brooke would say years later, was not his love language.

Both of Meyer's daughters sought affirmation from their father, perhaps in the way that Don Meyer used to listen through a heat grate in the hope that his own father would say something nice about him.

Brittney tried out for cheerleading in high school, mostly in an effort to get her father's approval. "I very much wanted him to like me, and I wanted to do the right thing," Brittney recalled. Over time, she created her own niche within the family through her humor; she was apt to say something that nobody else would say, and make the rest of them laugh—especially Don Meyer.

They came to view him as someone who could swoop in when it counted the most. He had always told them that if they ever had a major problem, just let him know and he would be there for them, and his daughters would indeed discover they could rely on him in a crisis—like when Brooke became pregnant while enrolled as a freshman at Lipscomb.

She had gone to her parents' bedroom to tell them, with Brittney at her side; years later, Brittney recalled feeling in that moment deep relief that she wasn't in Brooke's place. For Brooke, this was an excruciating journey for a daughter who above all else did not want to disappoint her parents—and given the strict doctrine of her church and the stature of the Meyers in the community, this would hardly go unnoticed. She would face a gauntlet of judgment.

Her father was fully supportive. "I've told coaches in clinics that you have to be prepared for something like this to happen," Meyer said, in a measured tone. He called the family doctor to set an appointment for her. "It's all going to be okay," he told her. Given the doctrine of the Church of Christ, Brooke had gone before the rest of the congregation and told them about her pregnancy; shortly after, she suffered a miscarriage.

Almost exactly a year later, Brittney had called Brooke and said, "You owe me one." Brittney needed her sister to accompany her to their parents' room, because Brittney, now a freshman, was pregnant. Carmen was furious; Don Meyer was calm, as he had been with Brooke, and supportive, telling Brittney that she would get through the crisis. Brittney, like Brooke, had gone forward in her church and spoken to the other members, asking for their prayers. "If you don't want to give them, that's okay," she said, her voice measured. "I'll be okay. I know God has already forgiven me." She left school, got a job, married, and in the fall, the first of her two children, Chase Finley, was born. She later had a daughter, got her degree, and remarried.

Brooke would marry and have four children, and when Meyer's phone rang at 6:30 A.M., Carmen and Don knew it would be Brooke, calling to check on them. Brittney would continue to be the one who made them laugh, and she and her father shared humor that might have been more common among college teammates. He would tease her about having a large head; she would make fun of his obsessive time management. Through adulthood, she had kept a written list of the most inelegant, blunt remarks her father had made to her, including something he said to her after coming out of surgery from a heart procedure years before his accident. "I know sometimes you think I love Brooke more than you," he said, "and you are right. She needs that. Mom loves you very much." At first, she had been stunned, but she wrote down his words and wielded them in her jocular jousting with her father. *Dad, remember what you said to me about Brooke . . . ?* It was something serious that had become something funny in their relationship.

Meyer adored Chase, his first grandchild. The toddler crawled around the floor of the Meyer living room as Don Meyer watched. "Brittney," he said proudly, "I can say something that few grandfathers can: That's one good-looking bastard."

Years later, Brittney would laugh aloud as she repeated this story. It was an example of Don Meyer's discomfort with emotion; intimacy for him was always easier when cast in humor. Both Brooke and Brittney cherished their father. And they had always wanted to hear more from him, and to be more deeply entrenched in his day-to-day life, which was a continual struggle. After Don and Carmen Meyer moved to Aberdeen, he returned to Nashville for a visit, and called Brittney to arrange a time for a meeting at Captain D's. When she arrived, there were members of his basketball team already sitting with him. It wasn't that she disliked any of them; she had just expected to have some time alone with her father, without basketball attached.

Basketball seemed to be embedded in Jerry Meyer, as it had been in his father. He had been a precocious child, and read and understood math much more quickly than most of his peers. He seemed like a basketball savant, having spent his childhood with his head ducked into the Lipscomb huddles. He spent hours at practices, listening to his father coach, watching.

One time, Jerry Krause, who had coached Meyer in college, flew into Nashville for a visit and, leaving the airport, he shared the backseat with Jerry Meyer, who was ten or eleven years old at the time. The boy started firing basketball questions at Krause—the way that his father had years earlier—and Krause was stunned by how sophisticated the questions were. The boy had to be a genius, Krause decided, because what he was saying reflected a level of knowledge that a lot of adult coaches didn't possess.

Fifteen years after Jerry Meyer played college basketball, Randy Baruth went through copies of Jerry's notebooks that his father had kept, and Baruth could see the court vision that his father always talked about. Within the notebook, Jerry explained how he had been in a situation when he saw a teammate open down the floor—and if he flipped the ball one-handed, in a manner that was not sound fundamentally and would probably anger his father, he could get the ball to his teammate. But if he brought the ball up and made a two-handed pass, the opportunity would be lost. Baruth saw that Don Meyer's son was aware not only of his own responsibilities and where his teammates were on the court but also where the opposing players were. This was the rarest combination of vision in the sport.

Jerry Meyer would become an outstanding baseball and basketball player, and the most nervous that Don Meyer could ever remember feeling about anything was while watching Jerry pitch. In time, he saw his son's need for perfection; he had to be good at everything. Jerry put a lot of pressure on himself. He wanted to be the best student, the best athlete, the best at everything, his father thought. "As his parents," Don Meyer would say years later, "I'm sure we didn't help with that."

Jerry joined David Lipscomb's basketball team for the 1989–

90 season, and while he had played on a team of senior stars, he quickly became the steering mechanism for that team. He had a knack for sensing in a given game what the team needed, and for providing what was lacking. Jerry might score two points in a game, but somehow dominate play on both ends of the floor. Don Meyer tried to objectively assess his son's performance—and thought that Jerry was the best player he had ever coached, in terms of his level of execution. By the time he would finish his college career, Jerry Meyer would have more assists than any player in college basketball history.

But his relationship with the David Lipscomb coach was far different from his teammates'; they collaborated, and they clashed. The other players diligently took down everything Don said in their notebooks, but there were times that Jerry didn't even bother, feeling like he had heard everything before. Don Meyer, concerned about the perception among the other players that he might treat his son differently, yelled at Jerry like the others, but maybe a little louder. And while the other players could walk away from a tense practice or game and separate themselves from Meyer, Jerry and Don had to go home together. Brooke always felt for Jerry. "With Brittney and I, we were competing against his players," she said, "but they were guys. We had something different than they had. Jerry was one of the players, and I can't imagine how hard that was for him."

It was always difficult for Jerry, Carmen Meyer thought, "because Don had a lot of sons. Jerry wasn't really his only son."

One game when Don Meyer screamed at Jerry, Wade Tomlinson—a senior trying to help a freshman cope with a barrage of criticism—went over to Jerry and said, with profanity attached, "Don't listen to [him]." And when Tomlinson later reflected on the moment, it dawned on him that he had been speaking about Jerry's father, and how blurred the lines must have been for Jerry—and for Don Meyer. At halftime, Don Meyer would pause momentarily in his preparation for the second half to check the box score to see how many assists Jerry had, as other parents would do. Then he quickly reverted back to coaching mode.

"We always talked about sports," recalled Jerry Meyer, years later. "That's our bond. I don't think we're that much different than most fathers and sons other than that I played for him, and I think anyone who played for their dad will tell you that it's a unique experience with a lot of complexity to it.

"It's hard. It's your dad, and all of a sudden he's in the coach role, and you're trying to win the game. He was an intense coach, I was an intense player. How do you go back to just being father and son? I think that's where the real rub is, and that was tough. It's one thing for a coach to yell at you, but when it's your dad yelling at you for coaching things, it's not the coach yelling at you; you hear your dad yelling at you."

The added layers would permanently complicate their communication. Before Jerry Meyer's senior season, he had violated team rules and Don Meyer kicked him off the team—a moment that Don Meyer spoke of often when holding coaching clinics in the years that followed. He advised the men and women in the room unequivocally: If you have a choice, do not coach your own children. Never talk basketball with your child unless you have a whistle on, he counseled, meaning that there should be a wall between what takes place at the gym and in home life. If he had to do it all over again, he would have tried to ensure that home was a quiet place for Jerry, separate from basketball.

The price that had been exacted in the relationship between Don and Jerry Meyer manifested sometimes as Jerry grew into adulthood in silence. When Jerry and Don Meyer were together with other Lipscomb players in a social setting, it felt awkward to the others. Jerry Meyer had married and had two children, and Don recognized the strong relationship in place between Jerry and his kids; Jerry had learned how to be a dad, Don Meyer thought, without the best example.

Jerry and his family had been eating Mexican food when the call came about his father's accident, and in the hours that followed, he felt numb and overwhelmed. Once he, Brooke, and Brittney landed in Sioux Falls, they took a cab to the hospital. When they arrived, Carmen greeted them with hugs and said, "I've got something to tell you."

Their mother explained how the doctor had found carcinoid cancer in their father's liver and small intestines. She then brought her children to intensive care, where, some medical staff had explained, their father was certain to be unconscious, still recovering from surgery. His neck was in a brace. He had a breathing tube in his throat. Spattered blood covered parts of his head. They could see the bruising forming on his badly swollen left side. His shattered left leg, stabilized with a rod, was covered almost entirely with a cast, except for his toes, which were pale blue.

His breathing was labored and erratic, but he was peaceful. It was the first time any of them could remember seeing their father—a man who was always on the move, always successful, always working, always in control—as vulnerable.

And he was awake, somehow, his eyes open.

He couldn't speak. Meyer wriggled his right hand. One of the Meyer children mentioned aloud that he seemed to be indicating that he wanted to write, and Meyer grunted in assent. Jerry placed a piece of paper underneath his father's hand, and a pen was placed in his palm. Meyer began writing, slowly, with his right hand, the words scrawled but legible.

How long before I can coach?

He indicated he had more he wanted to write, and Jerry turned over the paper. He wrote:

I luv you. I am proud of you.

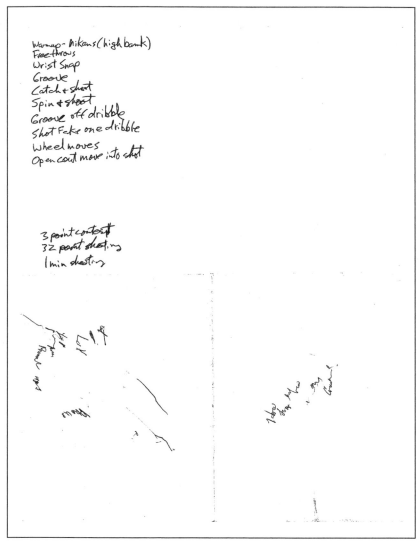

Warmup - Mikans (high bank)
Free throws
Wrist Snap
Groove
Catch & shot
Spin & shoot
Groove off dribble
Shot Fake one dribble
Wheel moves
Open court move into shot

3 point contest
32 point shooting
1 min shooting

The first words that Don Meyer wrote (lower right corner) to his family the day after his accident: How long before I can coach?

CHAPTER 6

Word of Meyer's accident spread quickly. Brittney had called Barb Anderson, Meyer's assistant for eighteen years at David Lipscomb. Anderson immediately began dialing the numbers of Meyer's old players by memory, and one of the first she called was Wade Tomlinson, a shooting guard Meyer coached for four seasons, from 1986 to 1990. He had fallen asleep in the room of his young daughters at his Indiana home, and after his wife, Jennifer, handed him the phone, he had sat out on the stairs, stunned.

Tomlinson had known Meyer since Wade was in the fifth grade, when he first attended Meyer's summer camps, and while Meyer didn't easily betray his feelings, other players on the team thought that Meyer had a unique admiration for Tomlinson.

They recognized the similarities between Tomlinson and Meyer: Tomlinson had grown up on a farm—in Danville, Alabama—and like Meyer, he had driven a tractor by the time he was in the second grade and had been raised to work hard. When Tomlinson was a teenager, he noticed that the only time that his father would not ask him to work was when he was shooting baskets on the hoop at their house; Wade Tomlinson would make a point of dribbling hard enough that the echoes from the ball would reach his father in the barn. At David Lipscomb, he would ask Meyer each May for permission to miss the first part of the basketball summer camps to help his father with the planting of crops.

Like Meyer, he had drawn a lot out of his relatively modest physical abilities; he was six foot one and as skinny as a hoe when he started playing in college; he shaved for the first time in December of his freshman year. Tomlinson was genial and generally quiet, politely deferential. But Meyer demanded that he become more vocal and communicative with teammates, especially on the basketball court. There were times when Meyer would stop practice and penalize the players with push-ups when Tomlinson failed to speak up. One day, Meyer announced to the team that Tomlinson would do all the talking for all the players that afternoon; Tomlinson was the only player to speak. He was mortified, but adapted quickly, calling out anything that popped into his head. When you are a freshman and the seniors on the team are being penalized for something you failed to do, Tomlinson said, you make sure you change.

Numbnuts, Meyer called Tomlinson. As in, *Numbnuts here didn't call out the screen. . . . Just start running.*

Tomlinson spoke with an Alabama drawl, and wore his hair a little longer than some of his teammates, enough so that there was a swirl of blond curls. He wasn't supposed to play much as a freshman—in fact, there was some talk of redshirting him, giving

Wade Tomlinson shoots in front of the Lipscomb bench.

him a year of only practice before he would join the team for games—but Meyer had kept him on his active roster as a spare part. One night, David Lipscomb got locked into a close game, and one guard was out sick and a starting guard fouled out with about a minute to play. Tomlinson sat in his chair on the Lipscomb bench and saw Meyer—in need of a player at that moment—look at him, and then look elsewhere, and then look back at him. "Put in Wade," an assistant coach said to Meyer, and grudgingly, Meyer sent Tomlinson into the game. With time running down, a rebound was knocked loose to Tomlinson, who threw up a three-pointer that turned a two-point deficit into a one-point lead with seven seconds left. After Lipscomb won, Meyer sought out Tomlinson just before he met with reporters. "Make sure you talk about your teammates," Meyer said. "Say something nice about your teammates."

Meyer could be curt with players' girlfriends as well. During Tomlinson's senior year, he was dating Jennifer Jean, and Meyer saw her after a game. "Be sure Wade ices those knees," Meyer said, the only words he uttered to her before graduation.

Tomlinson devoted himself to weight lifting, creating strength, and as his chest and shoulders got bigger, Meyer would bark at him in practice that he was doing all this just for beach muscles. But in truth, Meyer admired his devotion to making himself a better player and to growing into a leader. Tomlinson might have been reluctant to talk as a freshman, but by his last years at Lipscomb, he had developed a strong voice on behalf of his teammates.

In the fall of Tomlinson's senior season, David Lipscomb was playing a controlled scrimmage against Aquinas Junior College, in which the coach of either team could stop the action to instruct his team. David Lipscomb was ranked number one in the preseason, but Meyer was particularly tense. In the midst of that scrimmage, one of the Bisons failed to step into the path of an opposing player driving with the basketball, and an infuriated Meyer called a time-out and told his players that none of them had the physical toughness to draw a charge from him, a forty-five-year-old man. Like Bear Bryant running a football drill, Meyer made the David Lipscomb players who were on the court line up and practice taking a charge, with Meyer acting as the offensive player and ramming into them with his shoulder. Jerry Meyer was the first and he tumbled back, and the others fell over like bowling pins.

Tomlinson was on the bench nursing an injury, but seeing Meyer challenge the players in that way inflamed Tomlinson, and so he stood up. "I'll take a charge from him!" Tomlinson snapped, cussing, and others on the bench had to physically restrain him from going onto the court; finally, they wrestled him out of the gym. "I'll take a charge from *you*!" he yelled.

Meyer had always growled at the players that when they wanted to quit, they could just leave their basketball shoes in their lockers, and in this instant, Tomlinson yelled that he was quitting and threw each of his shoes. But Meyer—whose players had always thought he was a little hard of hearing—had his back turned to Tomlinson, and either didn't hear him or chose not to hear him. An assistant retrieved the shoes before Meyer saw them. Tomlinson was at practice the next day, of course.

There were times, after practices, when he would go back to his dorm room and smack his pillow, imagining that he was punching Meyer's face . . . and enjoyed it. But at the same time, Tomlinson realized that Meyer's criticism was on the mark. "There's this deep internal respect that I think all the players had for him, no matter how aggravated or mad or frustrated they got, because they know he's right," Tomlinson recalled. He came to think that this was part of the process of evolving from a boy into a man—a teenager's feeling of invincibility and self-importance gradually honed into a young adult's perspective on mistakes and accountability. "He was great in reminding you—life's not all about you," Tomlinson said. "If you want to be happy in life, you'd better learn to serve others."

Tomlinson finished his career with 1,792 points, but beyond that, he left the program with special status bestowed upon him by Meyer. Philip Hutcheson, one of Tomlinson's peers, first noted the seemingly superhuman powers of their predecessors— the guys who had played for Meyer before them. Meyer held them up as extraordinary models of effort, of execution, of achievement. Meyer spoke of them with such reverence, Hutcheson said to his teammates, that they were like the Super Friends, referring to the TV cartoon. One night, the Lipscomb players had sat up and matched the Meyer graduates with characters from the show. Ricky Bowers, a player that Meyer respected, clearly was Superman. Bob Ford and Richard Taylor had to be Batman and Robin, because Meyer never mentioned one without the other. "It was always, 'Bob and Richard,' 'Richard and Bob,' " Tomlinson recalled.

After Tomlinson graduated, he became one of those held up by Meyer as an unattainable god to Meyer's latest generation of players. Tomlinson remained deeply loyal to his teammates after he moved to Indiana and started a family with his wife, Jennifer. In his daily work, Tomlinson found himself relying on words that Meyer had said during practices and in the team meetings, mantras that Tomlinson had written down in his notebook or that had lodged in some corner of his brain.

Don't let your greatest strength become your greatest weakness.
Do the right thing the right way at the right time.
If ya ain't what ya is, ya isn't what you ain't, so you ain't what
  you are. In other words, be yourself.

If you wrestle with a pig, you're going to get muddy and only the pig enjoys it.

He came to believe that Meyer had probably been the best possible person to usher him and his teammates into adulthood, someone who had made him believe that excellence was obtainable if he did things the right way, and that failing to do the right thing was not an option.

Tomlinson would drive to Nashville to go to David Lipscomb to visit Meyer and the others in the Bisons basketball program, bringing Riley Jean, his son, when the boy was just one year old. When some of his former teammates started coaching themselves, it was typical for Tomlinson to show up to their games unannounced. He once drove two and a half hours to see a game coached by Jason Shelton. "Hey, I wasn't doing anything today anyway," Tomlinson said, after Shelton thanked him. The Bisons talked all the time, like a band of brothers.

Tomlinson called Shelton on the first Saturday of May in 1999. Initially, Shelton could not understand the words that his old friend was saying; he was incomprehensible. Shelton was able to slow him down. "My boy is gone," Tomlinson said softly. "My boy is gone."

Earlier that day, the Tomlinsons had realized that Riley was out of sight, and in the frantic search, Wade Tomlinson had raced to a neighbor's pool, to which there was a small opening that spring, because of construction. He saw his son at the bottom. Wade Tomlinson administered CPR and he later told Shelton that, for a moment, the boy's eyes opened—and then closed.

Meyer and Shelton drove to Indiana immediately. When they came through the door, Jennifer Tomlinson greeted them with a hug and thanked them for coming. "I'm okay," she said. "Wade needs you." Tomlinson was on the floor, in a fetal position, moaning.

Meyer and Shelton reached down to him. At that moment, Jennifer Tomlinson recalled years later, Meyer was the person that Wade Tomlinson most needed. Tomlinson needed comforting, and Meyer—who had probably had the greatest influence of anyone in his life—was the person who could do that.

Hour by hour, Shelton saw Tomlinson emerge from his deepest grief, as others of his former teammates arrived, as they began telling the old war stories from the days they had played together. One day, Meyer took a long walk around the neighborhood alone with Tomlinson, and when they returned, Shelton thought Tomlinson had reached a point of equilibrium. Meyer, however, was more shaken than he let on; he was almost overwhelmed by seeing Tomlinson so devastated. Tomlinson had asked Meyer on their walk whether he thought it would be right for Riley to have a basketball jersey in the casket.

Meyer and Philip Hutcheson took care of the memorial service for the boy. Wade Tomlinson stepped forward to the casket and read a book to his son.

When Meyer spoke, he talked about how families faced with traumas like this often broke apart. It was a good thing, he said, that Wade and Jennifer had the tools to stay together. "You need each other," Meyer said in the church. "You have to help each other."

More than three dozen former David Lipscomb players— many of whom did not play with Tomlinson—attended the service, and when it was over, Meyer gathered the young men he had coached. It is a time like this, he told them, that distinguishes you.

For years afterward, friends and neighbors of the Tomlinsons would recall how exceptional Meyer's tribute was that day. Jennifer Tomlinson thought back on what Meyer had said and knew the coach was concerned about how the young couple's marriage would survive the tragedy. In the months that followed, Jennifer Tomlinson could see her husband slowly emerging from his pain, but there would be days when he seemed to drift emotionally, when he'd fall into emptiness. She'd call Meyer. "I'm right on it," he'd say, and a minute or two later, she would hear Tomlinson's cell phone ring in some other part of the house.

In retrospect, Tomlinson wasn't sure if he would have been able to stick with the marriage if not for what he had learned playing under Meyer. "I don't know what kind of family guy I would be," he said. The death of his son was "really hard to get over—you never really get over it—and I'm really thankful for the things that I learned."

It wasn't long after Riley's death that Tomlinson approached Meyer at a summer basketball camp. "Coach, I can't thank you enough—" he said, but Meyer cut him off. "Wade, we *all* can't thank each other enough," Meyer said. "I can't thank you guys enough for how you helped me. If you want to thank me, go do something for somebody else."

Tomlinson listened. He decided to make a point to talk to others about loss, about its depths, the depression. "As bad as you get," Tomlinson said, "as bad as you feel, you survive."

The front of the Tomlinsons' refrigerator was sprinkled with little cards that Meyer had sent, and Jennifer Tomlinson would hear her husband talk to their two daughters and instantly recognize phrases she knew were inherited from Meyer: *Girls, the only things you can control are your attitude and your effort.*

But now Meyer was badly hurt and Tomlinson wasn't sure what he could do. "Wade," Jennifer Tomlinson told him, "you need to go."

At 1:30 the next morning, Tomlinson walked into Avera

McKennan Hospital in Sioux Falls, South Dakota, not knowing whether Meyer was alive. He braced himself for what he would see, but the vision of his badly bruised coach, attached to tubes, was still jarring. Meyer had blood on him, and the doctors had told Carmen Meyer and her children that it was still not clear whether Don Meyer would live.

"Hey, Coach, Numbnuts is here," Tomlinson said, his voice light.

"Wade . . ." Meyer said, his voice barely a whisper.

Tomlinson continued to joke, as he often did with his coach.

"I love you," Meyer said.

Tomlinson knew this. But he was sure that nobody who played for Meyer would ever believe that their coach had said it out loud.

CHAPTER 7

In Meyer's first days in the hospital, others asked what he could remember about the accident. He told them that he recalled looking ahead for the turn to the hunting lodge. Then he remembered a flash of white—presumably, he said, this might have been the air bag as it deployed. And he told family members that he recalled being above his own car, floating, so that he could see himself sitting, while Brett Newton and Kyle Schwan, his players, shouted at him to stay awake and keep his focus. Meyer remembered the people helping him.

He clung to life in those first days, his condition still serious, and it was the first time that Jerry Meyer could recall seeing his father this vulnerable and open. Some of that, Jerry thought, was probably due to the medication, which seemed to be affecting him like truth serum.

But part of Don Meyer's openness, his son believed, was because he was bedridden and forced to focus on those around him in a way he had not when basketball was in season. It was good to hear the words of affection, Jerry Meyer thought, but it was uncomfortable, too, because he and his father had never really interacted like this. Jerry would internally process these conflicting emotions for the next weeks and months.

Jerry decided to bring his two young children to Sioux Falls, and when Don Meyer saw them, he was touched by the gesture— and the thought crossed his mind that Jerry wanted to make sure his father connected with his kids at least one more time in his life.

His condition did improve, hour by hour, but even as he got better, a weight hung on the family, because they knew what he did not yet know—that he had terminal cancer. Meyer was still fighting to survive, so the doctors continued to ask Carmen Meyer and her children to keep the news from him, as an emotional blow could devastate him.

Meyer was keenly aware of how fragile his own condition was. His chest was badly broken, and he struggled to wheeze out thoughts one or two words at a time. His first words to assistant coach Randy Baruth and to Brenda Dreyer, the school's director of university relations, were an apology. And he paused to tell them he loved them. "Make this . . . good for . . . the school," he said to Dreyer.

Meyer told Dreyer to take out a notepad to write down a list of messages that he wanted to get to certain people. These were meant to be final sentiments in the event that Meyer died suddenly, Dreyer realized. She wrote quickly in her notebook, fighting back tears, trying to keep up with his personal testaments.

On the third day after the accident, Northern State assistant coach Randy Baruth and Jackie Witlock drove from Aberdeen to speak to Carmen, and to ask her for permission to tell the players about Meyer's cancer. Meyer was well-known in the area and reporters were asking questions, and Baruth worried that somehow word about Meyer's cancer diagnosis would get out, whether through a nurse or a friend of a friend. He did not want the players finding out that information secondhand.

Carmen agreed, and as Baruth spoke to the players later that night, he felt especially pained for them; the players had gone to Northern State to play for Meyer, specifically, and now they were being told that not only was he battling life-threatening injuries that they had all witnessed but also that he had an illness that would eventually take his life. After everything these kids had gone through—all the resilience they had shown—Baruth just wasn't sure how much more they could take.

The players were summoned to a small classroom not far from Meyer's office at the Northern State gym, expecting Baruth to give them an update on Meyer's condition. Just before the meeting started, Baruth pulled sophomore Casey Becker to the side.

Becker had decided to attend Northern State because of Meyer. His sister had played basketball at the school, and while Casey Becker was still in high school, he had traveled across South Dakota to watch Northern's women and men's basketball doubleheaders and had been taken by Meyer's coaching style. Becker was good enough to play college basketball, and he saw no benefit in going to a school where the coach was going to promise him playing time or try to be his best friend. He wanted to get better as a player, and as a person. When Meyer had spoken to Becker during the recruiting process, he had been direct and, most important to Becker, he had been honest. He told Becker that he needed to get quicker, that he needed to work on his shot. Becker knew that if he was going to play at Northern, he would have to challenge himself physically and emotionally.

The son of two schoolteachers, Becker wanted to play for Meyer, no matter how much money he was offered in a scholarship. He felt he would learn, one way or the other, and that he would be a better person after going through the program. Even if it meant paying for it himself.

Baruth lowered his voice so that the other players wouldn't hear his conversation with Becker, and he told him that the reason the meeting was called was to inform the players that Coach Meyer had carcinoid cancer. He wanted Becker to be prepared for the news. Becker walked into the classroom in an emotional haze.

Baruth then told all the players, working off some notes he had prepared. He informed them that Meyer had cancer; he did not tell them that doctors had talked about a possible life expectancy of two to three more years. He told them to stay together, to use this to make the team stronger. The players were silent at first. Kyle Schwan, who had attended to Meyer in the moments after the accident, was overwhelmed. Meyer was a rock for them all, Schwan felt, and none of it made any sense.

Kevin Ratzsch, one of the team's two seniors, was the first player to speak, and his words were filled with hope and resolve. "This is why the accident happened," he said. "So they could find the cancer." The exact same words that Carmen Meyer had uttered to Baruth the night of the accident.

The players talked about remaining positive, for one another and for Meyer. The meeting ended, and the players went to work out together, Becker among them. For him, there was no doubt that Meyer would be back. "I just knew that he wouldn't let something like this stop him," Becker said later. "I knew that he wouldn't just want to give in." Becker already was hearing speculation within Aberdeen that Meyer might have to walk away from basketball. Telling someone like Meyer that he might have to hang it up, Becker believed, would spark a fire in him.

After a brief trip home, Brooke Napier returned to Sioux Falls on September 11, the day before Meyer was to be told about his cancer—carcinoid cancer, a slow-growing cancer that is typically difficult to diagnose, because it can often be present for years without presenting any symptoms. Dr. Strand, the trauma surgeon who had worked on Meyer in his first night in the hospital, had found a number of tumors in Meyer's liver and small intestine.

While at home in Nashville, Brooke had tried to gather as much information as possible on the Internet about carcinoid cancer. She took pages of reports with her on the plane, and fought to keep her composure throughout the trip. When she arrived at the hospital, her father greeted her cheerily. "Brooke, I am so happy to see you," he said.

The next morning, Strand told Carmen Meyer and her daughter that now was the time to tell Meyer about his cancer; if they waited too long, Strand said, then Meyer might never completely trust the doctors again.

Brooke Napier assumed that there would be some kind of meeting to discuss how her father would be told the news, and that she and her mother might be given some sort of preparation on how to help him in the aftermath. But Strand was direct and said, "Let's go." Carmen was partially relieved to be telling her husband; she had been fearful all week that a nurse or therapist would mention the diagnosis inadvertently.

Carmen and Brooke were in the room as Strand explained to Meyer how he had found the cancer. He did not specify what type of cancer it was, or that carcinoid cancer grew slowly. After Strand departed, Carmen explained what the doctors had told her.

Meyer broke down for a few minutes. They all cried.

"I'm okay," Meyer said eventually. "It's just a lot to take in."

Quickly, he regained his composure. He was aware of the emails and cards and calls that had been pouring in, and that the South Dakota press was following his progress in the hospital. Meyer's nature was to be direct. He turned to Brooke and said, "We need to put out a statement." And she took down his words:

It is now ten A.M. on Friday, September 12. My trauma surgeon, David Strand, just told me they found carcinoid cancer in my liver and small bowels. The cancer was discovered during the emergency surgery after my wreck on September 5. What's great about this is I would not have known about the cancer had I not had the wreck. God has blessed me with the one thing we all need, which is truth. I can now fight with all of my ability.

"What I now ask is that everybody who believes in God would praise Him for this discovery and pray to Him to give me the strength, patience, and peace to be a man of God on this journey. I am looking forward to coaching this season and am forever thankful to my team who saved my life and the coaching staff, which has stepped up to the plate.

Meyer had coached for almost four decades, and in that time he had pushed his players to demand excellence of themselves, to handle trauma with accountability, and to answer challenges aggressively and gracefully. Do not dwell on things that you cannot change, he had told his players; focus on the next best action. Do the next right thing right. And now, after being told he had an illness that would probably take his life, Meyer reacted as he had counseled so many of his players to react. *Keep alert. Stay calm. Do not be afraid.*

Baruth had been standing outside the door, having sleeplessly worried about how his mentor would react to the terrible news. But as Baruth came into the room and saw Meyer seizing the moment, responding so strongly, he felt a surge of pride; Brooke Napier had a similar reaction. Her father had lived out his own words.

CHAPTER 8

For decades, Meyer had run youth basketball camps, with as many as five thousand kids participating over the course of a summer. To facilitate instruction, he would bring in dozens of high school and college coaches, many of them young coaches just starting out. He'd arrange for houses for them to sleep in, and through the years, many would stay in the Meyers' guest rooms or basement. After the Meyers purchased their house at Northern State, the place was renovated to add three bedrooms, a bathroom, and a living space in the basement, where coaches would stay for free.

Meyer had also hosted annual clinics for coaches, and hundreds would come in to hear Meyer or guests like John Wooden,

Jerry Sloan, and Tubby Smith. Meyer produced and marketed a series of basketball videos, with Meyer and his players demonstrating and teaching on camera, that had sold well for over twenty years. Because Meyer had coached his entire career below Division I, he was not known to casual basketball fans. But in the circle of coaches, he was renowned because of his teaching style and willingness to help other coaches.

Pat Summitt, the all-time leader in coaching victories in Division I, met Meyer while coaching at his first camps as she began her career at the University of Tennessee. She felt intimidated by his brusqueness at first. But Summitt saw how good Meyer was at getting his point across with the players; they understood exactly what he wanted them to do. She liked his focus on execution, on how you catch the ball and place the ball, the drills with the guard play and on entry passes into the interior of the defense. For the rest of her time as coach, she would keep pages and pages of notes that she had taken at the Meyer clinics, and hired one of her assistants, Dean Lockwood, based on Meyer's recommendation.

One time she found Meyer going through her organizer, to see how she prepared for each day. "There's something special about him," Summitt said. "People gravitate toward him, maybe because of his sense of humor, or because he's incredibly bright. I love him like a father."

Bob Starkey, an assistant coach for Louisiana State, went to one of Meyer's clinics in the early nineties to listen to Meyer, and was struck by the depth and openness of his basketball lectures. Starkey had grown accustomed to the high degree of secrecy in college basketball, where many coaches protected information used within their programs like national security documents. Meyer, on the other hand, invited him into his office to look through his notes and pamphlets and handouts and take what he wanted. "If you need something, just grab a copy," Meyer told him. Starkey quickly realized that Meyer treated *all coaches* this way—really, anyone who had interest in basketball. Through the years, Starkey filled three file cabinets with handouts and notes from Meyer's program.

Starkey and Meyer became friends, the two of them chatting on the phone, trading notes or laughs. After Starkey sent him something on a colorful LSU letterhead, Meyer sent Starkey a note on a sheet of paper ripped from a spiral notebook, with its flaking edge tattered.

Bob
This is Division II stationery.
Don

There was a time when Starkey was trying to cut down on sweets. Meyer pulled out a package of Oreo cookies and offered Starkey some. "I can't have that," Starkey said. "I'm on a diet."

"Bob," Meyer said flatly, "I don't like to snack alone."

Starkey, laughing, turned down the offer again.

"Bob, your wife is not going to know," Meyer continued. "You will have some and you will enjoy them."

Starkey declined again. A week later, a small box arrived at the Starkey home, addressed to his wife. Inside was a package of Oreos and a note from Meyer.

Bob left this in my briefcase. Please return it to him.

The Louisiana State women's program went through a difficult time in 2007 when head coach Pokey Chatman resigned. Meyer called Starkey every day, asking him about Pokey, giving him advice, and Starkey came to realize that he was one of dozens of coaches that Meyer communicated with in this way; Meyer had basically adopted a generation of coaches.

Starkey found Meyer's accessibility to other coaches remarkable, given the level of the success of his programs and his camps. Meyer's phone would ring and a high school coach would be on the other end of the line, taking Meyer up on his standing offer to talk basketball, and the coach would present Meyer with some particular quandary he or she was having—with a defense, or how to run an inbounds play, or how to deal with an issue that had come up with one of the caller's players. For Meyer to take calls from a young coach, in the world of coaches, was like Bill Gates taking phone calls from an up-and-coming computer programmer.

Meyer didn't care much about how he looked—to him wearing a button-down collared shirt was like dressing up—and while he was generally organized, he wasn't a neatnik, given the various piles stacked in the corner of his office. But his script, on a piece of paper, was incredibly precise; he wrote letters the way an architect draws structures, with sturdy bearing walls and solid foundations and well-crafted curves. And as an extension of that, he had spent his life assessing pens, for their execution of the elements of letters, for how they felt in the hand, for how freely or stiffly the ink ran out of them. He could be in the middle of a conversation and, in mid-sentence, reach over and pull the pen out of a visitor's hand and then write out a few words in the same way that a golfer might reach into the bag of a friend and feel the heft of a driver. Years before, he had been at Starkey's house and picked up a gel pen, swirling it across a piece of paper. "Bob," Meyer said, very seriously, "this is a *great* pen." Starkey had found a box of the pens and sent it along, and Meyer had loved them.

In the days after Starkey heard of Meyer's accident, he thought about this. Starkey sat at his computer, and on a rectangular card that had two pictures of Meyer, he wrote a message to basketball coaches:

On Friday, September 5, legendary coach Don Meyer was involved in a serious automobile accident. While his prognosis is good we are looking for coaches to rally around this special person and show him the love and encouragement he has shown to us. PLEASE TAKE THE TIME TO "PEN" YOUR THOUGHTS TO COACH MEYER AND THEN MAIL HIM YOUR PEN!

The address for Meyer's office was included on the card, along with two pictures of Meyer and a picture of a fountain pen, and the cards were sent out in a mass email to the coaching community. Starkey dropped a fat purple Louisiana State pen into an envelope and sent it along to Meyer.

The letters and pens began arriving at Northern State University in waves, in letter-size envelopes, in manila envelopes. Each day, Susan Entzel, the secretary at the athletic department, would walk the mail back from the student center and then stuff Meyer's in-box, and when there was no more room in the in-box, the letters were stacked in front of it. Ryan Hilgemann, the basketball team's manager, stood at Meyer's empty desk with the coach's silver letter opener and went through all the mail, shoving all the packages and letters that appeared to have pens into a massive clear plastic garbage bag, to take to Meyer.

The letters came from coaches at Connecticut and Colorado, from Tennessee and Texas, from Alaska and Alabama, from Florida and Arizona, from Massachusetts and Rhode Island, from states in the South and the North and the Midwest and out West. Hundreds and hundreds of letters, from elementary school coaches and former coaches and middle school coaches and high school and college coaches.

I recently had the chance to listen to you speak at a clinic in Louisiana this past summer. You made a huge impression on me at a time when I needed it most. . . . I know that you had a purpose to be at the clinic to speak to my heart. So I owe you a great deal for that. . . . I had never met anyone that impressed me more than my own dad and I think I found someone to run a close race (please don't tell him that)—you are awesome, inspiring and a holy man, and I pray for your full recovery.

Ashley Brodhead-Richard, St. Thomas More Girls' Basketball, Lafayette, La.

Don:

My thoughts and prayers are with you and I'll be pulling hard for you as you face these challenges.

You have always been a great inspiration to me!

Roy Williams

The University of North Carolina

One of my classes is Introduction to Coaching Team Sports, and last Thursday, I showed my class one of my favorite videos, "The best things I've seen in coaching." My class was very captivated by you and enjoyed what you had to say about being a successful coach. Get well soon, Coach, my class and I are thinking about you.

Bryce Newell, Whitney High School, Rocklin, Calif.

Coach Meyer,

I got a chance to listen to you speak a few years ago in Evansville, Ind. I have always thought a lot of you as a coach and as a person. I've also learned a lot about coaching and working with young people from you. Thanks for being a blessing in my life.

Sincerely, Jason Powers

[Apollo High School, Owensboro, Ky.]

Don,

Just wanted to tell you everyone at MSU has you in their thoughts and prayers. You've been great for both the game of basketball and the game of life! Thanks for all you've done. Please work hard and get back and continue to share with all the great knowledge you have.

Tom Izzo
[Michigan State men's coach]

My thoughts and prayers have been with you. You're special to me!

God Bless,

Pat

[Pat Summitt, the University of Tennessee]

Arizona State's Herb Sendek sent a note, and so did Florida's Billy Donovan and Bill Self of Kansas, and many, many others. A letter arrived for Meyer on Texas Tech stationery—from Bob Knight.

Meyer had come to know Knight through their work at clinics and revered his ability to teach basketball. He felt that Knight simplified his instructions in a way that players could understand. Meyer's own style was similar to Knight's in that both demanded that their players focus, to the point of fear. One time, Meyer and his team had gone to visit Knight's team at Indiana, and Knight invited all of them into the Hoosiers' meeting; Meyer had always been deeply appreciative of that. Not many coaches or players had been inside a meeting of Knight's team.

Knight had seen Meyer's drive when he had first met him in the 1970s. "I remember very early that I thought, *Here's a guy who wants to become as good a coach as he possibly can be,*" Knight recalled. "In fact, it kind of reminded me of the way I went about it when I first started."

Meyer asked questions of Knight—direct questions to draw information and clarify some point about how to attack a zone defense, how to break a press. Knight came to view Meyer as "an extremely good coach. Now, I don't say that about a lot of people. He really worked at the game of basketball. His teams were very fundamentally sound, they played the game the way it should be played. I felt that he was a guy that really wanted to teach the game of basketball, and not just coach it. And there's a difference. I always felt that if I was an athletic director in one of the major athletic conferences, he's the first guy I would've talked to about trying to come with me."

Meyer was in bed when his daughter Brittney handed him Knight's letter, in which was enclosed a pen. Like a kid systematically opening a Christmas present, he first made a point to try out the pen, with a swirl of ink. "Nice pen," he concluded, before handing it over to Brittney. Then he read Knight's letter to himself, twice, before reading it aloud to the others in the room.

> *Dear Don:*
>
> *I can't begin to tell you how sorry I was to learn of your car accident you were involved in and the injuries you sustained. I sure hope you are improving daily and want to wish you the very best for a complete recovery.*
>
> *I hope you enjoy the pen I have enclosed.*
>
> *Best wishes.*
>
> *Sincerely, Bob Knight*

"That's a great letter," Meyer said, emphatically. "Isn't that a great letter? Every word means something. That's a great letter."

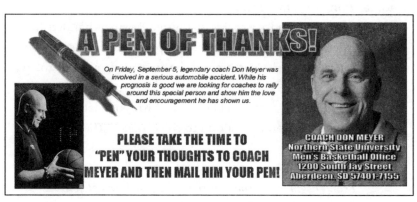

The flyer that Bob Starkey sent out to the coaching community.

CHAPTER 9

Meyer's cancer was something hidden, with no apparent symptoms. But Meyer's left leg was wrecked, and doctors endeavored to save it. Meyer made it clear to them, in his first days in the hospital, that he could accept amputation, if necessary. He felt lucky to be alive, and responsible for the accident. If he lost some of his left leg, well, perhaps that would be his penance. "Doc, just cut it off," Meyer said at one point.

Meyer's wounded leg became infected, and the pain overran the defenses of the morphine administered to him. Surgery was scheduled for September 19, and doctors told Meyer that during that operation, they would determine if the leg could be saved. If not, Meyer's leg would have to be amputated just below the knee.

The night before the surgery, Brittney was in Meyer's room, trying to make him feel more comfortable. He had terrible pain in his neck from the accident, and Brittney climbed between the bed and the wall to get an angle to rub his neck. Her father started sobbing.

Even if his leg was saved, he knew he would be looking at months and months of therapy, with more rounds of surgery. The leg was shattered, losing muscle, and it was unknown how well it would heal or how functional it would be. "If I come out of the surgery with my leg," Meyer said to Brittney, weeping, "I don't think I could do this." His leg hurt so badly, and he was overwhelmed by the thought of trying to rehabilitate a leg that might not even be useful to him.

His daughter absorbed his words and thought: *He's going to be okay if his leg is amputated. And he probably needs to have the amputation.* The next day, his left leg was amputated about eight inches below the knee. The surrounding tissue was swollen, badly inflamed, raw, an open wound, the calf hanging down. To Carmen, it looked like a steak at a meat counter.

In the months ahead, the cancer became almost an afterthought. Carmen and Don had sat together as a doctor had bluntly briefed them on the extent of the cancer. It was inoperable, and all that could be done was to treat the symptoms as they developed, with shots of hormones. When the meeting was over, Don had turned to Carmen and told her that in the future, he could not participate in any more conversations like that. He did not want to hear about the cancer. What he wanted was for Carmen to speak to the doctors, gather all the information, and then tell Don where he needed to be for whatever treatment was needed—rehabilitation, shots, whatever.

His more immediate challenge was living without his left leg, living with the pain, and learning how to walk again. Those challenges would be inherent in almost everything he and Carmen would do for the rest of his life.

Right after he was moved out of intensive care, he had a day when he felt completely overpowered by the enormous challenge that lay before him, and as Carmen Meyer saw the depression in her husband, she was deeply affected and would remember that very blue day for months.

The next day, Don Meyer apologized. "I'm sorry I had a bad day," he said. "We've got to take this one day at a time."

"You're exactly right," Carmen replied.

Dr. Jonathan Stone had worked in rehabilitation of patients when he had moved to South Dakota in the summer of 2003. But more and more, he focused on pain management, on trying to help patients deal with their pain without simply going for the quick fix of drugs. He had first met Meyer before his amputation and noticed that the coach asked very specific questions; he wanted to know the reason for everything—not to question the competency of the doctors and nurses, but to understand the process. Meyer was now able to write in his notebook again, and he seemed to write down everything: the plans for the day, his schedule, thoughts about what was going to happen. And occasionally, Dr. Stone said something that might be useful in coaching, and Meyer would write that down as well. "I've got to remember that one for the players," he would say.

Sometimes the wounds of an amputee can close relatively quickly. If the wound is covered, there is less stress on the sensory nerves, so the patient has less pain. But Meyer's wound remained open for days and wouldn't close completely for months. The sensory nerves that had been severed were hypersensitive to any stimuli—touch, a change of dressing, even air. The resulting pain was extraordinary.

Any open wound needs to be kept moist, so the dressing covering the amputation won't become embedded and need to be pulled away from those nerves. Ridges and peaks and valleys of damaged nerves appeared at the end of Meyer's left leg, and as the dressing on his amputated leg was removed for the first time, the pain was unlike anything he had ever experienced before. Despite being heavily medicated, Meyer started yelling as the dressing was removed.

Dr. Stone positioned himself behind Meyer and wrapped his arms around him and held him, partly for physical support, and partly for emotional support. Stone wasn't sure if he had ever seen anyone in as much pain. Meyer began singing—almost shouting—a hymn that popped into his head, a hymn that he did not remember singing before; it wasn't until weeks later that Meyer looked up the words.

> *To God be the glory, great things He hath done;*
> *So loved He the World that He gave us His Son,*
> *Who yielded His life an atonement for sin,*
> *And opened the life gate that all may go in.*
> *Praise the Lord, Praise the Lord,*
> *Let the earth hear His voice!*
> *Praise the Lord, Praise the Lord,*
> *Let the people rejoice!*
> *O come to the Father, through Jesus the Son,*
> *And give Him the glory, great things he hath done.*

Carmen wasn't familiar with the words either, but somehow, they emerged from her, and she sang along with her husband in his agony. Afterward, she was convinced that the spirit of God had moved them in that moment, together, to help ease his pain.

Day by day, the agony of the dressing change diminished; and day by day, Carmen Meyer tended to her husband. He could see flashes of her competitive side. She kept track of what was said about his left leg and his cancer, and as they met with various doctors, she would correct the physicians about some past development or the timeline. Dr. Stone came to know Carmen as well as her husband. On one hand, he felt, there was a Southern belle side to her: She was beautiful and her years in Nashville had left her with a trace of a Southern accent. On the other hand, she possessed an unflinching resolve in her personality.

Carmen Meyer collected animals for her grandchildren. Dead animals. This was something her daughters teased her about and found a little morbid. But the science fascinated Carmen Meyer, the manner in which God put together the bodies of creatures like puzzle pieces. She found a dead garter snake and cut it open so her grandchildren could see the rib cage. She found a skull of a small bird, its beak extended majestically. She found the front teeth of a squirrel. She found a small tree trunk that had been cut by beavers, and cut off the trunk and carefully placed it in the plastic bag, along with the wood chips that had fallen to the base of the tree. The Meyers' garage had a slight smell of dead animal, because that is where she kept the zoo of skeletons.

Like a naturalist, she was fascinated by how bodies worked, how the skeletal structures linked together. One day she saw a dead coyote in the road near where the Meyers live, and the next morning, as she and Don drove to church, the coyote was still there, intact, in the middle of the road. She asked her husband if he had any interest in helping her collect it, and he gave her a look, eyebrows raised: *Not a chance.* So after she dropped her husband off at home, she returned with a large garbage bag and collected the coyote. She struggled to lift the body into the back of the van. She removed the tail and hung it with the other items she saved for her grandchildren, and put the rest of the coyote behind the garage.

It rained for a week straight, and when she went back to look at the carcass, she discovered that the hair and meat were coming off the bones easily. Through an Internet search, she learned that she could dismantle the coyote and preserve it. Piece by piece, she took apart the coyote and boiled it down to the bone, laying out all of the bones on towels on her kitchen counters to dry. During the process, she discovered that inside the coyote, there were smaller bones from smaller creatures—a rabbit, perhaps, or a small rodent. She sorted all the bones into plastic Ziploc bags, separated by different parts of the body. All the teeth and the jawbones were together, the small and large vertebrae were together, all the small bones of the feet were together. She found great wonder in all this, like a doctor, and sometimes Don Meyer mentioned that she would have been an exceptional surgeon.

Or maybe she simply had the kind of faith through which she felt she was doing the right thing in respecting and honoring what she saw as God's work. Her brother J.D., who had been playing cards when Don visited her family's house for the first time, had Down's syndrome, and nobody in the McCune family asked why; they merely saw all that was good and great in him. Now her husband was crippled, and she set her mind to caring for Don, to helping him recover. She did not leave the hospital until he was better.

The nurses showed her how to change Don's dressing and clean his wound as her husband looked at the ceiling, unable and unwilling to look at the blood. A friend popped by when Carmen was changing the dressing one day, and Carmen nodded toward her husband's averted eyes. "He's such a wimp," she said, shaking her head and smiling. And he admitted: Guilty as charged. Carmen is the tough one, he told visitors.

When their jobs and family situations allowed, Brooke and Brittney returned to Sioux Falls, sharing the care of their father. He could not move and could not care for himself, and his family helped the nurses with the most basic of care, cleaning, helping him function, swabbing and applying ointment. Meyer found great relief in having his neck and foot rubbed, and Brooke and Brittney did whatever they could.

The language that their father used in the aftermath of the accident was not something to which they were accustomed, and it was for that reason that Brittney began to view his time in the hospital as a gift. "I didn't want to see him suffer, I didn't want to see him go through what he did, but he was really able to express himself," she recalled. "He was able to use words like 'wonderful' and 'tremendous' and 'excellent' and it would be about the smallest things. It would not just be about basketball; it was about me, it was about my children, it was about my husband, it was about my ex-husband. He wanted people to know how he felt about them and it was great."

They all felt needed in a way that they never had before. Their conversations with their father had often been casual, partly because he was distracted by some issue with the basketball team. But in the hospital, there was an entirely different focus, a different depth to the conversations. "He spoke to what really mattered," Brittney recalled, months later. "There was no telling what he would tell you, when you were sitting in the room with him. He probably told you a lot of things that maybe he had always been looking for his dad to say to him."

Once Meyer told Brittney, "The most important thing you can do for your kids is to be there for them." The words might have been built on regret, she knew, but he also meant them as a compliment to her, because Brittney had always been there for her children. He and Brooke talked about spiritual things, to help him keep his mind focused, as she rubbed his hands and foot. Brooke thought he was "ooey-gooey sweet." Even if this openness was partly due to his medication, the words were wonderful for her to hear, a confirmation of the love she had always felt but rarely heard expressed.

Meyer's family began to view the accident very differently from the way they had initially. Already, it had borne blessings for them. The newfound intimacy, Brittney thought, might never have occurred were it not for the accident. Caring gestures might not have been extended. Meaningful words might not have ever been spoken.

Brittney felt it a gift as well to see her father's interaction with the hospital staff.

Mindy Voss had worked as a registered nurse at the hospital in Sioux Falls for six years, in rehabilitation. She wasn't much of a sports fan and hadn't heard of Don Meyer; she hadn't even heard of Northern State University. But there was a lot of talk about him among the staff members at Avera McKennan before Meyer was admitted into her section of the hospital.

The morning that Meyer was rolled in, he asked the others in the room to leave, because he wanted to talk with Voss alone. The room emptied, and Meyer reached out for Voss's hand. "Will you say a prayer with me?" he asked her.

From that point forward, Voss felt a connection with Don and Carmen Meyer, because of their spirituality, because of the way they treated the staff and the patients. She found them sincere and earnest, interested in helping those around them. Voss burned an Alan Jackson CD of hymns for the Meyers, specifically to listen to during the dressing changes. Jonathan Stone felt the same kind of connection; he, like Voss and other staff members, would swing by the room where Meyer lay, to talk, to hear one of his corny jokes, or to pray. He spoke to different staffers about one of his favorite passages from the Bible, James 3:13–18:

> *Who is wise and understanding among you? Let him show it by his good life, by deeds done in the humility that comes from wisdom. But if you harbor bitter envy and selfish ambition in your hearts, do not boast about it or deny the truth. Such "wisdom" does not come down from heaven but is earthly, unspiri-*

tual, of the devil. For where you have envy and selfish ambition, there you find disorder and every evil practice.

But the wisdom that comes from heaven is first of all pure; then peace-loving, considerate, submissive, full of mercy and good fruit, impartial and sincere. Peacemakers who sow in peace raise a harvest of righteousness.

They called him Coach, and it wasn't long before many of them wore Northern State basketball T-shirts to work; he had had Randy Baruth, his assistant coach, bring down boxes of the shirts, along with boxes of the pamphlets that he gave to other coaches about how to handle life's challenges and about the pursuit of excellence. The Meyers were assigned two rooms, 2–135 and 2–136, to help them with the overflow of boxes, mail, and visitors; the second room became a sitting room for those who had flown in. Staff members brought their kids to the hospital on their days off. What he did when he was in the hospital, Voss said, was coach a lot of the people who worked there.

Richard Taylor, one of Meyer's former players, visited during the first month, and it occurred to him that Meyer had essentially transformed his room into an extension of his office. Carmen Meyer had cut a long stripe of yellow butcher paper, about six feet long and four feet high, and hung it on the wall opposite her husband's bed. On that paper were written mantras and messages to himself, reminders about what he should focus on, as well as specific reminders about his rehabilitation.

YOU GOTTA KEEP DANCIN'.

STAY AHEAD OF THE PAIN.

DO THE NEXT RIGHT THING RIGHT.

Meyer was in physical therapy in Sioux Falls for almost two months.

Each day tested Meyer's stamina in different ways. Richard Taylor was there when Meyer had to go through both physical and occupational therapy. He was asked to lift himself out of his wheelchair and then stand on one leg, to work on his balance, an exhausting series of exercises for somebody who had been in bed for a month. And then, in occupational therapy, he worked on stacking cups. In the middle of that, Meyer simply nodded off in his wheelchair.

The therapist woke him immediately. "Okay, Coach, let's finish these drills here," she said. Meyer complied, quietly.

The next day, the same physical therapist was on duty when Meyer rolled in. "I had a dream about you," Meyer said.

"Really?" she said.

"Yes," Meyer said. "I had a dream that you were on your knees praying to God for forgiveness for what you did to me yesterday."

And then Meyer smiled. He jokingly said that the physical therapists were actually "physical terrorists." At one point, a therapist had pushed him in a way that was probably a lot like the way he had pushed his players, commanding him to action with one sharp word: "WALK!!"

Brooke and Brittney provided updates on Meyer's condition and rehabilitation on a website called Caringbridge, and one day Brooke noted that Meyer was going through some grueling physical therapy.

Someone in the email chain of Meyer's former players chimed in. "What I'd give to be HIS physical therapist," wrote the player, and this drew amused responses from those who understood exactly what he meant.

Brooke's kids—Don Meyer's grandkids—arrived at the hospital for a visit, and afterward, nobody could remember exactly the first time that he referred to the stump at the end of his left leg as Little Buddy. But he had done so initially to help the young children deal with any anxiety they might have about his disfigurement. "Can you say hi to Little Buddy?" he asked, and they said hi and then asked Little Buddy questions, to which Meyer would either nod yes with his stump or shake sideways for a no. His right leg, inevitably, was called Big Buddy. But Little Buddy became the favored son in conversation, the celebrity twin of the Meyer legs, a temperamental sort who needed attention. Forever after, Meyer referred to his stump in the third person.

> *Little Buddy is itchy.*
> *Little Buddy isn't feeling too good.*
> *Little Buddy likes that.*

It wasn't long after one of Brooke's visits with her children that, while working in her Nashville home, she started to hear the tearing of paper in another room. Shortly thereafter, one of her boys emerged from the bathroom completely nude, except that he had covered his most private of parts with Band-Aids. "See, Momma, I've got a Little Buddy too" the boy said cheerfully.

Some of the Northern State players visited. Matt Hammer had played for Meyer and returned for this season as a graduate assistant, which was why he had been in the caravan on the day of the accident, and in many respects, he found Meyer to be the same as always. But, like Meyer's family members and other former players, he found Meyer to be much more open. Meyer told Hammer he loved him, and for Hammer, this was touching.

Meyer said the same to Kyle Schwan, one of the team's seniors. "Kyle, I've got many sons," he said. "If I had to write a book, that's what it would be called: *I've Got Many Sons.*"

Doug Dodge, another of Meyer's former players, came to visit and told Carmen Meyer, "That was the best four hours in my life with Coach."

Wade and Jennifer Tomlinson's young daughters made get-well cards for Meyer. One of them had colored in a bloody accident scene—a picture that was inappropriate to send, Jennifer Tomlinson decided, except that the recipient was Don Meyer and he would get a good laugh out of the child's imagination.

Coaches arrived. U.S. senator John Thune visited. So many people came from Aberdeen that a schedule was prepared for visits. Mindy Voss, the nurse who had grown close to the Meyers, watched all this, saw all the cards and letters and pens. She thought the outpouring was extraordinary; it seemed to her as if the rehabilitation ward at Sioux Falls had become home to royalty.

One visitor held particular significance to Meyer—Don Carda, who had driven the semi on the day of the accident. After decades of pulling hay across the Dakotas, he was in his fourth year of retirement, but on that day he was doing some part-time work, hauling 66,000 pounds of corn along County Road 20. He was headed to Aberdeen to meet his wife, Reva, for dinner.

He saw a rise, and a car came over the top of that. A Prius. Its wheels were on the yellow line; the car was drifting into his lane. Carda's first thought was that the driver of the car had fallen asleep, something Carda had seen a few years before when a car had crossed the yellow lines and veered in front of him, barreling over the shoulder and into a field.

But at that moment, the Prius drifted into his lane gradually. Carda tried to slow down his rig, but the gap between the semi and the car closed too quickly. Carda turned his steering wheel slightly toward the right, drawing the semi onto the shoulder—but there was nowhere for him to go. And Carda thought: *C'mon, buddy, wake up. C'mon, wake up. Pull it over.*

He had attended Northern State basketball games, and to see Meyer pinned in his car had been crushing for Carda; the accident had badly shaken him. The semi that he had driven that day sustained $35,000 in damage, but after it was repaired, Carda didn't want it back; it would evoke too many awful memories, he felt. He got a different truck.

In the first weeks after the accident, the Northern State basketball players had invited Carda to team functions, where their presence could be of some reassurance to him that there had been nothing he could have done to avoid that collision with Meyer. After Meyer moved to the rehab ward, Don and Reva Carda drove the two hundred miles to see him. Reva Carda had made a blanket for Meyer with a pheasant on it. Meyer took the blanket and wrapped it around himself as if he were freezing, and they all talked, chatting about farming.

On October 15, basketball practice began at all NCAA-affiliated schools, including Northern State. Carmen and her children had been cognizant of that date, and how torn Meyer might feel on that day. Meyer spoke to Baruth regularly, talking about practice and about what the team had worked on, about the progress of each of the players. Basketball was the greatest lure for him as he went through his rehabilitation.

Meyer was told in late October that he would be released before the end of the month, and he was set on rejoining the team immediately. Northern State had exhibition games scheduled at the University of Minnesota on November 6 and at Purdue on November 8, and their first regular season game was set for November 18. Meyer diligently worked through his rehabilitation therapy, and the carrot in front of him, always, was his return to basketball, to his players. When he went through his daily rehabilitation, he was doing it in order to prepare himself to return to what he loved to do, not just to get better.

Dr. Jonathan Stone was skeptical that Meyer would be able to do all that he expected to do as coach; he really hadn't given himself a chance to recuperate. Stone thought that Meyer would find his recovery to be more difficult than he anticipated. But after a month getting to know Meyer, he also believed that nobody could dissuade him from going back to work. Meyer wanted to coach, and he would have to learn his own limitations on the job.

On one of Meyer's last nights in the hospital, he broke a two A.M. silence. "Carmen?" he said.

"Yes?" she replied.

"I can't wait to go to practice," he said.

"That's great," she said. "Can we talk about it tomorrow?"

At about eleven A.M. on October 30, 2008, fifty-five days after the accident, Meyer sat in his wheelchair in the hallway at Avera McKennan, and signed the paperwork for his release. Some of the nurses wore Northern State T-shirts. When someone asked him if he could push himself along in his wheelchair, he smiled and tucked the pen inside his shirt collar. "It'll be slow," he said, "but I'll get there."

Using a crutch, Meyer carefully lifted himself out of the wheelchair and slid into the front seat of the car that Jackie Witlock had driven from Aberdeen; Carmen hadn't been home since the accident. Another patient asked, "Coach, are you happy?"

"I'm thinking about it," he said, smiling slightly. Meyer's eyes were full of emotion as he looked back at the staff and waved slightly. Carmen steered the car away from the hospital and toward home.

Carmen phoned Brooke, who was driving her son Zev to first grade in Nashville, to let her know that her father had just been released. Brooke hung up the phone and burst into tears.

"Mama, what's wrong?" her son asked.

She was happy that her father was getting better, but she was not yet ready to give him back to the basketball team as she had in the past. "I'm just sad," she replied, "because Grandpa's leaving the hospital and I'm scared he's not going to need me anymore."

Brooke called her father, who assured her this would not happen. He would always need her, he said.

CHAPTER 10

A few weeks before Meyer's release from the hospital, he lay on the bed at the hospital one day during his rehab, surrounded by women. Six of them. They were members of Carmen Meyer's Bible study group, from different churches, and they had driven the two hundred miles to Sioux Falls to see Meyer and to pray for him. They held hands around Meyer's bed and everybody in the room closed their eyes, including Meyer. Amy Kessler, speaking in a strong and even tone, led the prayer.

Before she finished, however, Meyer opened his eyes and looked around, studying the determination and earnestness in each face. And this thought occurred to him: The Devil was in trouble that day, matched against these South Dakota women.

He had strong allies in the community now, but Don Meyer had been an outsider when he arrived in Aberdeen in the summer of 1999. He had come with a reputation for success, but with his social bluntness and sideline demeanor, he tended to make first impressions like a sledgehammer.

The Northern State basketball team struggled in his first couple of seasons, winning just half their games. Some established players walked away from the program, unhappy with Meyer's demanding style. The locals in Aberdeen had grown accustomed to the Wolves playing with a run-and-gun offense, racking up lots of points; however, Meyer coached his teams into a completely different style: defense-first trench warfare. This was functional and yet about as attractive to watch as a manure spreader being hauled in first gear.

It didn't take long for the folks in Aberdeen to figure out that Meyer was not going to let others influence his decisions. He seemed too stern during the season, virtually unapproachable. A contractor had gone to the Meyer home to meet with Carmen about some remodeling, and word got around that Don Meyer hadn't even said hello. "I thought he was really a jerk," said Harley Mohr, an Aberdeen resident who regularly attended the Northern State games. Mohr didn't understand why Meyer had to yell at the kids; he didn't understand some of the goofy drills that he thought Northern did, like at halftime, when they donned practice tops for their work on the half-court offense.

Bob Olson, the Northern State athletic director who had hired Meyer, had anticipated that he might rub people the wrong way, initially; he had known Meyer when he was at David Lipscomb and understood his demanding personality. But he was also convinced that, in time, Meyer would prove a perfect match for Northern State as well as for Aberdeen. Olson thought Meyer would eventually put together winning teams, but he also thought that Meyer's work ethic matched that of the folks in Aberdeen. At heart, Olson believed, Meyer was a Nebraska farm kid now taking a job in a community built on agriculture and the values that Meyer had grown up with. Meyer would run the basketball program with integrity, and the players in the program would compete and conduct themselves with integrity.

After the second mediocre season, Meyer said to Olson that if he had another flatlined season, Olson would have to fire him. But Olson didn't give that a second thought, and slowly the locals' perception of Meyer changed. "Because of the kids he turned out," said Harley Mohr. They were great kids, the kind who played hard and didn't whine to the referees, who said "Thank you" and "Please." The kind of kids who made the place better. The kind of kids who would show up at Aberdeen's annual book trade and carry boxes and boxes of books—about 100,000 in total—at the outset of the event, and then carry out the leftovers at the end of the weekend. Mohr and his wife, Darlene, hosted dinner for the basketball team at their house during the holidays, and the players helped clean the kitchen and offered to wash the dishes after the meal. If there was a major community event in Aberdeen, the Northern State basketball players would be there to help. (Through Meyer's years as a coach, he had sometimes been the bane of his players' romantic relationships; the girlfriends of the players had constantly seen dinner or movie plans frustrated by the unexpected announcement that their boyfriends had been assigned the responsibility of working at a basketball clinic.)

In Meyer's third season at Northern State, the Wolves shared their conference championship in what was the first of seven consecutive seasons of twenty or more wins. During the 2004–2005 season, Northern State averaged 2,400 in attendance—second best among Division II schools in the country, a remarkable achievement, considering that Northern State is a small school, in a town of 28,000, in one of the least populated states in the country. The next year, Northern State drew an average of 3,900 per game and led the nation in attendance, a feat that the basketball program would achieve in two of the next three seasons as well.

As Harley Mohr, a building contractor and real estate appraiser, got to know Meyer better, he decided that he had never met anyone like the coach; Meyer seemed to fit so well in Aberdeen because of his honesty, because he was genuine. Mohr felt Meyer cared about people; he thought Meyer cared about him. Once, when Meyer was on the radio, he promoted an upcoming team cookout—the Wolfdog Festival—and told listeners that they could come down and get a burger or a hot dog. "Or you could do like Harley Mohr," Meyer said over the radio, "and just carry one in each hand." Targeted by Meyer's droll sarcasm, Mohr felt honored.

Mohr walked away from his conversations with Meyer feeling like he had learned something; Meyer seemed to have something to teach everybody. Dean Zimmerman worked in maintenance at Northern State, and when Meyer went over to get some nails, he showed Zimmerman a carpentry trick. He pounded a nail into a board and then balanced other nails on that nail, all the while telling a story that was inspired by John Wooden; the point was about love, about having balance in your life.

When Harley Mohr decided to donate the proceeds from the sale of sixty acres of prime hunting land, he allotted sixty percent of it to his church, and donated the other forty percent—about $14,000—to the Northern State basketball program. Meyer was one of those people, Mohr believed, who would have a lasting impact on the community.

After Meyer's accident, the folks in Aberdeen shared updates on Meyer's condition with the same interest and regularity that they talked about the weather. Mohr called Jackie Witlock constantly to ask, "How are things coming?"

As their friends and neighbors thought about the Meyers, they wondered how they could help.

Carmen had slept on the floor in the intensive care waiting room the first two nights, and then checked in to the Center Inn across the street; trekking back and forth, she stayed in Sioux Falls with Meyer every day he was in the hospital. Some women who had heard of Meyer's accident asked a mutual friend of Carmen's if it would be okay if they spruced up her hotel room a bit, and made arrangements with the hotel manager to do their work while she was with Don.

When she returned to her refashioned room close to midnight, she was stunned. The women had brought in all new bedding—fancy, plush sheets and new, fluffy pillows. A soft new rug on the floor. The towels were wrapped in ribbons. The women had placed a vanity near the sink, in which they arrayed Carmen's cosmetics. Fresh plants and flowers adorned the room. They had brought a mini-refrigerator, a microwave, a coffeemaker, and a CD player. They had left baskets of fruit, reading materials, and candles, and put new shades on the lamps. They had hung her clothes on padded hangers in the closets. The room had been transformed into something beautiful, Carmen Meyer thought, almost like home.

Back in Aberdeen, the strength-and-conditioning coach for Northern State University, Derik Budig, arranged for sixty members from the Fellowship of Christian Athletes group to meet at the Meyers' empty house. With trailers, trucks, and cars, they transported lawn mowers, weed whackers, and leaf blowers that had been mostly used to blow trash from between the seats at the Wachs Arena.

They started at four o'clock, with Budig assigning different teams of athletes to different areas of the property: A group of volleyball players would cover one side of the house, a group of football players to another side, and so on. Some mowed the lawn. Some trimmed trees. Some raked the fall leaves. Some climbed ladders to clean gutters.

They worked two hours, until dark—until the Meyers' one-acre property was spotless. Somebody ordered pizza, and they shared that, too.

Curt Mitchell had a deep connection with Northern State University; his great-aunt had been the very first student to enroll at the school, in 1901. So Mitchell, who operated Modern Woodman, an insurance and investments business in Aberdeen, contacted his parent company and asked for a $2,500 donation. Northern State matched that figure, and with this money Olson arranged to make the Meyers' home handicap-accessible.

A hydraulic lift that had been donated to the school was installed in the four-foot landing that led from the kitchen door into the garage; this would help Meyer get to and from his home. Twenty-foot ramps, wide enough for a wheelchair, were placed over the steps that led from the dining room into the living room, and from the living room to the hallway leading to the Meyers' bedroom.

After visiting Meyer in the hospital, Jackie Witlock realized that the bathrooms in the Meyers' home would have to be altered as well. So she and her husband went to the Meyers' and wrestled for hours with the toilet-seat reconstruction. "Coach," she told him flatly, "I think you want a professional for this job." But they had finished the work.

One day, it had occurred to Greg Wieker, who lived about two and a half miles from the Meyers, that perhaps their lawn might be in need of some care. So he loaded his mower onto his trailer, packed up his kids, and headed down the road. He liked sports and had naturally gravitated toward Northern State University, but he didn't know Meyer that well. He just wanted to help. His kids picked up sticks and raked leaves, and he mowed. He told his five-year-old son, Malek, that Coach Meyer had been in an auto accident and that he needed help. The night that Malek learned this, he changed the way he ended his prayers. "God bless Coach Meyer," the boy said. "I sure hope he gets better." And then he'd climb into bed.

For months, the elder Wiekers would tend to the Meyers' lawn, while the youngest tended to his prayers.

Every week that Meyer had been in the hospital, Nate Reede made the drive from Aberdeen to Sioux Falls to visit the coach, calling ahead of time to make sure that Meyer's schedule wasn't already full. One time, when Reede walked in, Meyer was on the phone with the governor of South Dakota, who was calling to check on the coach.

Nate Reede had shared some of Aberdeen's initial reservations about Meyer. But in the midst of his late father's five-year battle with colon cancer, Neil Reede had mentioned to his son how the seemingly unapproachable basketball coach—a man whom Neil had befriended—had made a point to visit him regularly at home. When Neil had said aloud that he couldn't continue the fight anymore, Meyer had encouraged him, counseled him, helped him.

Neil Reede had left behind money to build a suitable locker room for Northern State's men's basketball team, and his son had inherited the friendship with Meyer; in the months after Neil Reede's death, Don Meyer had stopped by the Reede house to talk with them and visit during an extraordinarily trying time in Nate Reede's life. Meyer became a friend and mentor. "He's a gift from God for me," Nate said. "I value him as much as any friend I've ever had."

During one of Reede's visits, Meyer told him how he felt

about him—as he had with so many others—words you filled a life's journal with, Reede thought. Meyer told Reede that there was no need for him to make weekly trips to Sioux Falls. But Reede continued to make the journey to see Meyer. He felt a strong sense of purpose to help, in any way he could, the man who had so deeply connected with his father, and with his father's son.

Dean Zimmerman, the maintenance man for whom Meyer had demonstrated his nail trick, thought of something that Meyer might like. Knowing of Meyer's appreciation for carpentry, Zimmerman picked out a block of one-inch oak stock in his home shop, a piece of wood a little more than a yard long. With a TV on in the shop for background noise, Zimmerman ripped the oak with a table saw, thinning it, and spent about a dozen hours in the evenings after work smoothing the piece. Zimmerman made a handle at one end, rounded and clear-coated it, and covered the bottom edge with a rubber tip. He found old copies of the *Aberdeen American News* containing stories about one of Meyer's milestone victories and wrapped his gift inside that paper. It was a cane, for his friend.

As the Meyers drove back to Aberdeen on October 30, Cindy Kraft—a family friend—prepared their first meal at home. In the past, she had provided dinners for the basketball players during holidays, once making three trays of pork loin and mashed potatoes, and chuckling at how the players had eaten just about every morsel she had laid out.

In the hours and days that would follow the Meyers' return to Aberdeen, so many neighbors and friends would bring over food that Carmen Meyer's second freezer would almost immediately become filled with pies and cakes.

Although incredibly grateful, Carmen became a bit overwhelmed by the waves of food, and so Cindy Kraft and another woman began informally organizing the community catering service for the Meyers: *Why don't you bring over the dinner on Thursday, because it looks like they're all set for Monday, Tuesday, and Wednesday.*

At about two o'clock on the afternoon of October 30, the Meyers' tan van turned into their driveway for the first time in fifty-five days. They were home; the meal that Cindy Kraft had prepared was warm and waiting for them.

CHAPTER 11

The morning after Don Meyer was released from the hospital, Carmen drove him onto the campus of Northern State University at 4:45 A.M. The Wolves were set to practice at 5:30 A.M. What he wanted, of course, was a return to normalcy. What he wanted was to go back to being a coach, teaching players, helping them to get better. He did not want special attention. Normally, Meyer kept his practices open to the media or anybody else who wanted to watch, but on this day, the Northern State practice was closed to the public. He wanted his return to be as understated as possible, a private time for him and the players.

But Meyer's return to the court was a momentous event for the Wolves, for anyone who knew the coach, and for Meyer. Derik

Budig, the strength coach for the athletic department, greeted Meyer as he rolled onto the court for the first time. Budig glanced down at Meyer and saw his lower jaw quivering with emotion; there were tears in his eyes. Budig leaned down and hugged the coach. "Good to have you back," he said. "I love you."

Brad Christenson, one of Meyer's assistant coaches, watched Meyer come out for the first practice and felt happy and relieved for his friend, knowing that he was getting back to what he loved to do. The Wolves had already been practicing for two weeks, taking direction from Randy Baruth.

Meyer rolled onto the court in a black wheelchair and the players formed a horseshoe in front of him, as they always had before the accident, sitting in chairs and taking notes. Meyer spoke briefly, softly; because of the injuries to his chest, Meyer could not launch his voice as before. The gymnasium acoustics that had always worked for him now worked against him, because the bounce of a ball or the squeak of basketball shoes obscured his weakened voice.

Meyer explained he would take some time to get re-acclimated, and that they should continue to work as they had in the first couple of weeks, under Randy Baruth. But the truth was that Baruth didn't know quite what to expect after Meyer got back. He wasn't sure how much Meyer would be able to contribute. He assumed that the coach's transition from an eight-week stay in a hospital bed to a demanding full-time job would be filled with unseen potholes. Baruth had seen his late grandparents struggle to get into and out of cars, and saw how a simple fall could be devastating; Meyer, he knew, faced a lot of hurdles, in spite of his relentless will and desire to coach.

But Baruth also felt it important to make sure that the needs of the players—the needs of the team—were met. Before Meyer's first practice with the team, Baruth met with Matt Hammer and

Don Meyer on his first day back at practice, October 31, 2008.

Mark Delany, two of the other assistants, and told them, "You guys have to keep an eye on Coach." Baruth wanted to make sure that, one way or the other, the Northern State players were being coached either by Meyer or Baruth. What couldn't happen was for there to be a coaching void. Baruth knew Meyer well enough to know that this would be the most important thing to him, more important than whether Meyer was in the middle of everything.

And Baruth wanted to be sure that there would be no inadvertent collisions involving Meyer. Baruth assigned Ryan Hilgemann, the Wolves' manager, to stay close to Meyer and make sure that no bouncing basketball happened to carom off Meyer's stump; Little Buddy was still badly swollen. Given the pain that Meyer was going through, this was one of the worst things that any of them could imagine.

That first practice began, and as Carmen Meyer circled the court on the track, walking briskly for exercise, Hilgemann followed orders. His assignment was similar to that of a Secret Service agent—he was prepared to throw his body in front of any basketball that bounced Meyer's way and, at the same time, he needed to be cognizant of the coach's sensibilities. Meyer didn't want anybody to feel sorry for him, and if he had known at the outset that Hilgemann was his practice bodyguard, he probably would have balked. Initially, Hilgemann found watching over Meyer simple, because he was pushing Meyer in the wheelchair. But Meyer quickly became adept at rolling himself, and he liked to park himself right under the basket, within a few feet of the part of the court on which bodies and basketballs flew all over the place. Hilgemann began standing next to Meyer, rather than behind him, so that he had the angle needed to knock a player or basketball away.

Meyer became focused on the action on the floor, and as the

practice moved to different parts of the floor, so did Meyer, and there were several instances in which he tried to turn—only to find Hilgemann standing in his way. "Get out of the road," he told Hilgemann repeatedly. If Meyer didn't know what Hilgemann was doing at first, the student knew it wouldn't be long before he figured it out. But Meyer never said a word.

Meyer mostly watched and took notes the first couple of days. However, at one point he seemed to rise up from the sitting position to try to project his voice. He was angry. "I could've gotten that rebound from this wheelchair," he shouted as best he could. Kyle Schwan, one of the team's seniors, heard this and smiled inwardly, thinking, *Coach is back.* There were other moments like this when the Northern State players saw Meyer's old intensity, and on some of those first days, he was able to get through the entire practice.

On Meyer's full week with the team, the Wolves took a long road trip to play exhibition games at the University of Minnesota and at Purdue. It became apparent to many that Meyer's return from the accident might be tougher than expected. The simple act of getting him onto the team bus required some work, because of the narrow opening for the door of the bus and because of the steep steps. Meyer had not yet built up the strength in his right leg to simply hop up the steps, so Hilgemann and others placed a strap around Meyer; some pulled him up the steps, others pushed, everyone moving slowly to make sure that this was all done safely. They put a blanket on his bus seat, with a pillow for Little Buddy.

On November 6, the Wolves played the University of Minnesota, and right away there were problems. As Meyer rolled past the band, a bass drum tipped over and fell against his stump. Meyer never complained out loud, but his assistants knew that he must've been in agony. Forever after, he made jokes about the incident, speaking about his stump in the third person. "Oh, Little Buddy was not happy about that," he would say. "Little Buddy was pretty upset about that."

During games, Meyer had always liked to hold his time-outs out on the court, away from the crowd, with chairs brought out for the players to sit in as Meyer spoke in front of them. But the floor at Minnesota was raised, and there was no way for Meyer to quickly get onto the floor in his wheelchair. Baruth told Meyer that they could hold the time-outs on the bench, in order to create a way for Meyer to be in the huddle.

However, Meyer didn't want to disrupt the team's routine, and he told Baruth to keep it the same. But this meant that during breaks in the game, the Wolves huddled while Meyer sat in his wheelchair to the side, not part of the conversation.

Carmen Meyer had made the trip, and after the game Baruth sought her out. "I don't like having the huddles so that Coach can't be in there," Baruth said. She agreed. "He's just going to have to accept that things are going to be handled differently," Carmen said. Thereafter, in those situations in which Meyer's wheelchair made it impossible to huddle on the floor, they just huddled on the bench.

The players adapted as well. In the past, Meyer could make his point to a player with a shout, but now, after the accident, the players couldn't hear him across the court anymore. So they started making a point of getting closer to him. If a whistle blew and there was a pause in the action and Meyer wanted to speak to a player, the player would glance over and see Meyer focusing on him, either in voice or gesture, and he would quickly run over to Meyer so that he could speak to that player directly.

In that first game at Minnesota, sophomore Alex Thomas came out a game and headed for an empty seat at the end of the bench but then heard Meyer's voice: "Al." Thomas moved directly in front of Meyer so that Meyer could make his point in a soft, frail voice. Very quickly, all the players took their instruction from him in this way.

The Wolves bused nine hours from Minnesota to Purdue for a game on November 8, and the others on the trip could see how drained Meyer was. When the Northern State team arrived at Purdue's arena, the bus driver wanted to move down to a loading dock ramp, from which the players and Meyer might easily make their way into the building. But a security guard would not let them enter, even after the staff members told them about Meyer's situation. "I'm just doing my job," the security guard said repeatedly.

So the bus had to be parked in a remote lot, and in a cold rain Harley Mohr, the Aberdeen resident who had made the trip, pushed Meyer completely around the building to get back to that same ramp where the security guard wouldn't let the bus park. Once inside the building, Carmen Meyer found an administrator and blistered him for what had happened. The players had always known Carmen as someone who was cheerful and supportive, and Randy Baruth thought that this was, for many of them, their first insight into how competitive and protective she was.

When Meyer came onto the court for the first time at Purdue, the student section rose as one and clapped for him. It would not be the last time this happened during the season.

Meyer was not so tender with the referees that game. Just before halftime, Northern State center Rob Thomas got hit hard on a shot, but the officials didn't make a call. Meyer was furious and wanted to confront them but couldn't get to them on his own. So he yelled to Matt Hammer, the graduate assistant, to push the wheelchair and head off in full pursuit of the referees as they tried to get back to their dressing room. Hammer and Meyer caught up to the offending official just before he walked through the door, and when he turned around, he did a double take. Hammer figured it was probably the last thing this referee had expected to see.

Meyer was still seething when he got into Northern State's locker room. "Those Big Ten refs are too chicken to make a call because they want to make sure they get hired by the school," he said, almost spitting in anger. The players loved it.

But the fourteen-hour trip from Purdue to Aberdeen was grueling. Meyer was dead tired, fighting the effects of his injury and his medications, and his handicap, and the first days that followed the trip were difficult. Baruth had to be ready to step in and provide whatever Meyer was not able to do on a given day. It was much less than an ideal situation, of course; with most teams, the head coach serves the role as the tough bad cop, and the assistants are the good cops who soothe, explain, and amplify.

With Meyer lacking his voice and stamina, Baruth had to work in both roles—sometimes he had to be the heavy in practice when Meyer could not be, and if Meyer did make a strong point to a player, Baruth had to revert to his softer stance. All of them had to adapt to a situation for which they had no training, for which there were no instructional videos. They would all have to do the best they could, under circumstances that none of them could have ever envisioned.

There were days when Meyer would come in and go through practice and be able to work into the morning. But there were also mornings when it was clear, after a few hours, that he just needed to go home, and Baruth would call Carmen Meyer and ask her to come and get him—to rescue him from his work ethic—because it was never Meyer's instinct to ask to go home to get the rest he needed.

In Meyer's second full week of practice, he rolled over to

Baruth in the middle of practice, handed him the practice plan, and rolled away from the court. Then Meyer stopped his wheelchair and started to cry. He simply was unable to get through the practice. Meyer went home for the rest of the day and after practice was over, Baruth returned to his own office, and closed the door. He called his wife, Meghan, and said through his own tears, "I don't know if he's coming back."

Late that afternoon, Meyer called Baruth on the phone, and they talked at length. Meyer had gone home and slept all day, exhausted. "Randy, I'm sorry," he said. "I've got some adjustments and changes that I have to make with this."

"Coach, you have to do what you have to do," Baruth replied. "If you can't be there every day, that's okay."

The next morning, Meyer was up early, as he was every morning. As a child, he would go to the barn before the sun was up, after his father or mother had called to him. As an adult, he deeply valued his time in the mornings. He was constantly refining his morning routine, trying to draw as much from it as possible. For him, the mornings were like filling a cup, preparing for the day.

This would be the time Meyer would read—the Bible, or whatever book he happened to be rifling through, marking important phrases with a yellow highlighter. It was a time for him to go through a prayer list he had maintained and updated for years. During his hospital stay, Meyer had once shown the prayer list to Jonathan Stone, his pain-management doctor, and Stone was stunned by its length—there were literally dozens and dozens of people on it, with various ailments and problems—as well as the meticulousness of Meyer's effort to pray.

Meyer placed a dot beside the names, as he prayed, and the names were organized, highlighted in different colors. Meyer also had an additional collection of emails, folded into his notebook, from others who had asked him to pray for them. He would pray alone, so that even his daughters weren't sure whether he prayed out loud or internally. After his prayer was over, Meyer reviewed his plans for the day, packed, and headed in to work.

The day after he had broken down during practice, he rolled into the Barnett Center, renewed again, his emotional cup refilled, prepared for practice. It was still dark outside. The Wolves' first regular-season game was only a few days away.

CHAPTER 12

Two days before Northern State's first regular-season game of the 2008–2009 season—Meyer's first regular-season game since the accident—a visitor drove him home from practice, pulling out of the parking lot of the Barnett Center at Northern State at about eight P.M. As the car stopped at a red light, a semi hauling two trailers had the green light and rolled harmlessly through the intersection. "I still flinch whenever a truck goes by," Meyer mused. "If we're on two lanes and the truck goes past, I still flinch."

A few minutes later, the car stopped in the Meyer driveway, and so began the arduous process by which he moved into his house. The walker that he used was unloaded by the driver and set next to the passenger's-side door, far enough away that the door could swing open but close enough that Meyer could reach out and grab it. Meyer swung his right leg and Little Buddy so that he was turned out. "Can you get my bag?" Meyer asked his visitor.

He pushed himself up onto his walker, and then hopped forward a couple of feet. After he moved far enough away from the car door, Meyer reached back and pushed the door firmly shut. And then, propping himself up on his walker, Meyer slowly moved from the driveway through the garage door, eighteen inches at a time, and up onto the hydraulic ramp. Once he and his visitor were loaded onto that, he popped a red button, and the ramp lifted him the two and a half feet or so from the garage floor to the level of the door that opened into the kitchen.

Carmen Meyer was there as he came through the door, cheerfully putting her hand on his shoulder; she was prepared to relieve him of any items that he might be carrying. "Watch your step," she warned.

Meyer moved carefully onto the six-inch rise that took him from the foyer and into the kitchen. He went through the kitchen, into the dining room, and then down a twenty-foot ramp into his living room. The surface of the ramp was rough like sandpaper, to prevent slipping.

Meyer pushed the walker to the side of his black leather lounge chair, and then eased his way into the seat. He was breathing audibly; he was exhausted. A journey that once took twenty seconds, without thought, now required five minutes and all the strength he could muster.

Meyer watched television and chatted for an hour, but it was time for Carmen to change the dressing on his leg. Meyer lay down in his bed, directed his eyes at the ceiling, and rested the stump of his left leg on a towel—another dark towel, which Carmen Meyer used because of the blood loss. She pulled off the sleeve covering his left leg. His triangular wound, with the flap of calf muscle and skin pulled over the front, was badly swollen and would not heal over for months. She pointed out for a visitor the small white spot inside the triangle. "There's the bone," she said.

She sprayed the wound with antiseptic and used a Q-tip to clean a fold of skin. "There's no blood here," she reported to her husband, a good sign. But he did not want to look; rather, he stared at the ceiling, his left hand over his forehead. More than two months after the accident, Meyer would sometimes find small bits of glass in his hand after running his hand over his scalp. The glass that had become embedded in his skin during the accident was still working its way out. His chest, Carmen would notice, was tilted slightly toward his right side, because the impact of the collision had been on his left side.

Meyer closed his eyes to think. He had another practice in eight hours, and his first game on the sidelines in less than forty-eight hours. This is what he loved doing. He loved coaching. He loved thinking about coaching.

His desire for knowledge about coaching had gotten Meyer into trouble when he was in college, playing for Northern Colorado. In the reference section at the library, Meyer saw a coaching magazine called the *Athletic Journal*. Meyer found the diagrams contained within the pages fascinating, so he cut them out and pasted them into a notebook that he kept—until he was caught, and required to refund the money for the cost of the mutilated magazines.

He had always known that he wanted to coach—indeed, he had informed George Sage, his college basketball coach, during his sophomore year that he would be a coach. Sage gave his players handouts to explain some piece of the offense or defense, or an inbounds play, and often, Meyer would come back the next day armed with questions. "I'd never had a basketball player who was so intent about learning all the intricate details about offense, defense, practice drills," Sage recalled.

While still a player, Meyer joined the theoretical discussions that the coaching staff had about basketball, like mathematicians talking about advanced calculus. In one of those bull sessions, the Northern Colorado staff and Meyer talked about how a team might handle a situation in which they had a two-point lead, with time nearly expired, and the opponent at the free throw line attempting one shot. The standard strategy for the team that was losing in that situation was for the shooter at the free throw line to intentionally miss the shot by bouncing the ball off the rim, so as to create a rebound and a possible attempt at a two-point field goal.

What the Northern Colorado staff decided, with Meyer involved in the conversation, was that the team with the lead could *intentionally step into the lane on every shot;* that way, if the player at the free throw line missed the shot, the officials would be compelled to call a dead-ball violation and give the shooter another attempt—making a rebound and a field goal impossible. If the shooter made the free throw, it would count for only one point and the team's lead was safe.

Not long after that, Northern Colorado was in the waning seconds of a game with a three-point lead and an opponent at the free throw line. The opponent's strategy was clear: make the first free throw, then intentionally miss the second and hope for a rebound and a field goal. Meyer looked at Sage and said, "This is the Step-In, Coach. This is the Step-In." The precise situation they had discussed.

Years later, Sage recalled, "I honestly don't know if I would've thought about it unless he had mentioned it." After the opposing shooter hit the first free throw, a Northern Colorado player intentionally stepped into the lane three times, flustering the officials, who felt as if they had no choice but to keep giving the shooter another try. With this strategy, there was no way Northern Colorado could lose the game. Years later, Sage remained astonished that Meyer had processed this so quickly. "By the time he was through playing for me, I knew he was destined to be a college coach," Sage recalled.

Jerry Krause joined Northern Colorado as a graduate assistant coach in the middle of Meyer's years as a player, and at his first practice, Sage told him to install an out-of-bounds play. Afterward, Krause found himself cornered by Meyer and another player. Both were wielding notebooks and pens, and quizzed Krause relentlessly about the play, about its structure, about its various options. Krause felt the questions were almost a litmus test, but he would discover that this was simply a manifestation of Meyer's obsession for detail. Weeks later, Krause was scheduled to make a recruiting trip to Nebraska just before Christmas, and Meyer asked him if he could get a ride back to his family's farm. For ten hours, Krause and Meyer talked nonstop about teaching and coaching.

Krause came to believe that Meyer viewed himself as a coach in the same way he thought of himself as an athlete. As a baseball player, Meyer was a pitcher who didn't throw hard, and as a basketball player, he wasn't fast, so he had to rely on his work ethic and attention to detail. In coaching, a relentless work ethic and ability to understand small details were powerful weapons.

With Sage's help, Meyer got a position as a graduate assistant and moved up the line, and in 1972, at the age of twenty-seven, Meyer was hired as the head coach at Hamline University, in Minnesota. Hamline went 5–20 in his first season, 16–10 in his second season. At a time with no shot clock in college basketball, Meyer coached in a defense-first, ball-control style. Krause was both impressed and concerned by the discipline that Hamline demonstrated: Meyer's team treated every possession of the basketball as if they were protecting nuclear codes—an approach that had to be constrictive for the players, Krause thought. "Everything you guys do takes so much effort—everything is a crisis," Krause told him. "You have to coach like you want to be coaching a long time. You guys act like there's no tomorrow. It's great that you want to learn; you can't exist over a long period of time coaching like that."

Meyer went to David Lipscomb College in 1975, and by then his overarching philosophy as a coach was established. For the rest of his career, he focused on trying to get his teams to perfect what they did—man-to-man defense, for example—rather than adjusting constantly to adapt to the strengths of the opposing team.

Rick Byrd of Belmont University probably coached against Meyer in more games than any other coach, and before every game against Meyer, he knew what offensive and defensive schemes Meyer's teams were going to run. But he also understood that Meyer and his players would execute so well and so efficiently that they would be successful even when their opponents knew what to expect.

Byrd knew, too, that Meyer's teams would be relentless in their intensity. They might have nights when they didn't shoot well, or when they didn't play effectively on defense, but they would always play hard, always dive on the floor for loose balls, always threaten to crush you if your players didn't match their level of intensity. Meyer's teams played with an admirable competitive arrogance.

Before Randy Baruth became Meyer's assistant coach at

Northern State, he had coached against Meyer, and what he realized in preparing was that Northern State never gave up easy baskets. Meyer stressed to his players Transition and Talk: Get back on defense quickly and make sure you talk with teammates about coverage. When opposing teams came down the floor with the ball against Northern State on a possible fast break, there were almost always at least two defenders in place, so that even a layup attempt would never be uncontested—resulting, at the very least, in a hard foul.

Meyer's strength as a coach, Baruth thought, was in the daily intensity that he imparted to his team—an intensity level that his players mostly learned to match—as well as his ability to identify the smallest fundamental flaws that prevented players from executing. If a guard missed a shot, Meyer would see that this player was not following through in his release of the ball. If Northern State failed in an attempt to double-team the ball handler, Meyer would diagnose instantly what mistake had been made and would tell the players—loudly, instantly—what adjustment was needed.

Jerry Meyer thought his father loved the process of finding solutions to basketball problems more than the games; it was as if Don Meyer were a musician who preferred the practice sessions in the garage to the concerts. He could stop practices and make the necessary changes. Correcting a jump shooter's technique. Finding the most efficient way for a player to help on defense. Creating a better inbounds play. Honing an offense.

Don Meyer focused on the process and taught his players to think more about the process than the results—but of course, he understood that a preponderance of correctly executed plays would almost inevitably lead to victories. A rival coach thought this was a brilliant method through which Meyer took pressure off his players: He relieved them of the big-picture worries about potential wins and losses by relentlessly training them to think only about what they could do better in any given moment.

What Meyer did far less than other coaches was focus on major in-game adjustments of tactics. If an opposing player got hot and was wrecking Meyer's team with his shooting, Meyer did not usually make significant alterations in the defense by switching to a zone or to some sort of specialized coverage designed to slow down that player, as many coaches do. This was partly due to Meyer's belief in his own system, Baruth thought. A rival coach once stood next to Baruth and said about Meyer, "You know what I like about Don? His attitude is: 'This is my team, this is what I do. Find a way to beat me.' "

Some of this was stubbornness, perhaps, and sometimes his teams probably would have been better served by making adjustments. This might have been a factor in one game which gnawed at him, in retrospect.

David Lipscomb had been ranked number one in the country near the end of the 1988–89 season, with a 38–1 record, and the Bisons were one game away from advancing to the national tournament—and that game was to be played in David Lipscomb's home gym, against archrival Belmont. But the game started badly for Lipscomb, because Belmont center Joe Behling scored twenty-nine points in the first half. During the intermission, Meyer told his players that Behling was "treed"—Meyer's phrase for a player performing beyond his seeming capabilities—and he assured his players that even if Behling was left unguarded, he couldn't possibly repeat his performance in the second half. David Lipscomb defended Behling the same way in the second half, and Behling went on to score exactly twenty-nine points in the second half. (This was a story that was repeated lightheartedly by his players for years, in the way that sons and daughters tell the turns-out-Dad's-not-all-knowing tales over

Thanksgiving dinner.) For years afterward, Meyer lamented that he had not made a quicker adjustment—and the next year, Lipscomb consistently played a defender in front of Behling.

While he tended to cling to his own team's philosophy during games, Meyer would nonetheless make major shifts to his tactics between seasons. David Lipscomb had played in a slow-down style in Meyer's first seasons as coach, but when the three-point shot was brought in to college basketball, Meyer shifted dramatically—and his became some of the most prolific scoring teams in history.

In that era, teams like Loyola Marymount and the Denver Nuggets popularized a run-and-gun style whereby the ball was rushed up the floor and jump shots were fired up almost without discretion—but Krause noticed that Meyer's high-offense teams were still built on the fundamental of looking for good shots inside, with the inside post man often then passing the ball outside for a teammate's three-point attempt. This style of play is how it came to be that the top two scorers in the history of college basketball both played center for Meyer. Philip Hutcheson set an NAIA record in 1990 with 4,106 career points for Lipscomb—and four years after Hutcheson graduated, his record was surpassed by the player who replaced him in the David Lipscomb offense, John Pierce, who scored 4,230 points and remains the all-time leader.

Lipscomb averaged 110.3 points per game during the 1989–90 season over forty-six games, and the 5,076 points the Bisons scored that year are the most for any team in college history. That record-setting 1989–90 team included Hutcheson; Darren Henrie, who finished with 3,004 career points; Wade Tomlinson, who netted more than 1,500 points; and Jerry Meyer, who remains the all-time leader in college basketball in assists for his career, with 1,314.

Don Meyer had an 891–299 career win mark as the Wolves prepared to begin the 2008–2009 season—good enough that he was asked to write articles for the publication that he had once cut up, the *Athletic Journal*. He viewed it as a penance for his college crime.

But as much as Meyer's passion for coaching and teaching had served as his carrot as he recovered in the hospital, Meyer had no idea if he would be able to coach. Before his first regular-season game, Meyer and assistant coach Randy Baruth didn't have a clear idea of how they would run the team from the sidelines. It depended on how much energy Meyer had, how much voice he could muster, whether he could contend with the noise of the crowd. There had been practices when Meyer's energy level was high, and on other days he had faded quickly. During games, he would need to be at his peak for almost two hours, nonstop.

He had rolled out to watch the Wolves warm up, sitting stoically, except when the occasional Northern State fan leaned over the bench to welcome him back—and then Meyer would smile and say hi before turning his attention back to the court. The National Anthem was played, and everyone in the gym stood to face the flag. Meyer, too: He pushed himself out of his wheelchair, and, using his right hand to balance himself, stood on his right leg.

After the initial jump ball, Meyer rolled out in front of the Northern State bench, leaning mostly toward his right in his wheelchair. He yelled out at his players as best he could. His voice was audible to the Northern State players when the team was on their side of the court, but he could not launch his voice in the way he always had. Immediately after whistles, players ran over to him, as had become their habit.

At the halftime buzzer, Meyer placed his handheld dictation recorder, which he used during games, into his shirt pocket. Assistant coach Mark DeLaney walked up behind Meyer and put his hands on the wheelchair, poised to push him off; Meyer, annoyed and not wanting any help in that moment of exasperation, immediately rolled himself away from DeLaney, heading back to the locker room and following his players for their halftime conversation.

Thirty-five seconds into the second half, Mount Marty's Justin Peters grabbed Wolves senior Kevin Ratzsch from behind by the jersey to prevent a breakaway. A foul was called, but not an intentional foul, and Meyer screamed at referee Ted Krize.

When Krize did not respond, Meyer—who did not typically berate the officials—called a time-out and rolled onto the court to pick up the argument, yelling from a distance. Krize listened, and nodded. Some of the Northern players thought Meyer was trying to make a point to the players: He was back, as intense as ever.

The Wolves won their season opener by forty-one points. Meyer spoke with the Wolves and met with reporters. He returned to his office, took off his tie, rolled toward his computer, and for a moment put his chin in his hand and closed his eyes. Meyer, just seventy-four days removed from his accident, was coaching again. He was exhausted.

A couple of days after that first game, the Meyers' living room was rearranged, with all the couches moved, in preparation for an on-camera interview. Meyer took a seat in front of the cameras, a microphone was attached to his shirt, and because of the lighting, Meyer was given a touch of makeup. "It's not going to help," he warned.

As he sat and waited, he turned to the interviewer and posed a question that he'd been thinking about. "Do you know," he asked, "if you could get charged with murder if you fall asleep at the wheel and hit somebody?"

Meyer paused for a moment. "If anybody else had gotten hurt, I don't think I would have made it out of the hospital," he mused.

When the interview started, Brittney Touchton sat on the floor just outside the room, listening to her father answer questions about the accident, about his return to coaching, about himself. She was curious, because he almost never talked about himself or his feelings, and on this day her father talked for more than an hour.

All Meyer could remember about the accident, he said, was "looking for the turn. Then all of a sudden, there's a big white pillow in front of me, which was the bags deploying. And then I'm spinning, and the guys were running at me yelling, 'Hang on, Coach, hang on, Coach.'

"And those guys were loud. They were real loud. They were yelling at me, shaking me and stuff like that to keep me awake."

Meyer was asked about his rehabilitation in the hospital. "I just wanted to get back as quickly as I could get back," he said. "I just wanted to get back with our guys. And that's a terrible thing to say—it sounds like I don't love my family. But my family was going to be there, I knew. If what you do is coach, you gotta coach. . . . I think it's what kept me going. That, and my family, and all the former players and friends that never let me spend a night alone."

Meyer said he prayed a lot in the hospital. "Sometimes you just pray for your family; they're going to take care of you, and you know how tough that is. You pray that you can be back coaching, with your guys. You pray that you can get to the next surgery. And you pray *with* people. That was one of the best things for me to accept."

His comeback, Meyer said, was a big challenge, "because I like to do things by myself. I like to let people go and let them work, but I like to watch what they're doing, too. I like to be able to out-work the people I work with and that's tough right now, because I can't put in a sixty-hour day.

"Right now, I have doubts I can coach effectively. Because if I can't do it effectively, then I don't think I can stay. I've got to evaluate honestly. I've got to make some decisions here at the end of this year, or two years down the road."

The interview stopped momentarily as the cameramen changed videotapes. The lights went back on, and Don Meyer talked about Carmen. "We've been married for forty-one years, so you never say it's always been sweet. And we're both pretty stubborn. . . . But we had to really work together through this and she's so smart, and so tough. And she doesn't miss anything. We went to a meeting with the doctors, and she corrected four doctors on things they were wrong on.

"It's been great for us to be together like this. I know I've disappointed her a lot of times, but she's always overlooked it and just plugged along. She's been a great mother, a great grandmother, and a great wife."

Meyer spoke at length about each of his children, about the memories he had of each of them as children. Going through the accident, he explained, had drawn the family closer together. "I hate that you have to go through an accident to do it," Meyer said. "But I guess that's sort of what we did with ours.

"I hate that everything happened. I wrecked and damaged the cars and the trucks. Fortunately, nobody was hurt. But it was a blessing. You read about angels in the Bible, but you never think about it. Probably there might have been an angel hanging on to me."

Meyer was asked why he loves basketball. His lower jaw began to quiver, and tears filled his eyes. "You play the game when you're a kid," he said. "You want to be great, you want to play professionally, and then you're not good enough, so you have to do something else. So you coach—and then you really get lucky because you work with kids.

"And I love to see how a team can improve and kids improve. So that's why I coach. I mean, there's nothing better than that. It just eats you up inside how lucky you can be to coach.

"I've never really taken a vacation," Meyer continued. "I never really enjoyed a vacation; I'm always thinking about working. If it wasn't a forced vacation, I wasn't going anywhere. And my family was there all the time for me in the hospital. It was a blessing in a lot of ways for me. It made me a different person.

"You're going to look at things differently. You're going to get emotional. You're going to cry a little more. You're going to hug people, you're going to want to say what's important to people before they leave. Because you might never get a chance to say it."

The lights went off, and Brittney walked into the room and hugged her father, who was exhausted. "Way to go, Dad," she said.

Derik Budig was in his eighth season as strength trainer at Northern State, working with athletes in all of the programs, and it would be his responsibility to help Meyer through his daily physical rehabilitation sessions. Budig wanted to be sure that he didn't push Meyer too hard. On one of Meyer's first days back, Budig saw him roll his wheelchair over near a wall next to his office, lower his cap, and fall asleep instantly. After a two-hour practice, Meyer was physically spent.

Each day, however, Meyer would make time for the rehabilitation sessions that he had started in Sioux Falls. He would lie on a long table and Budig would help him stretch, raising his legs to his chest fifteen times, in sets of three. In the midst of some of the exercises in those first weeks, Budig could see Meyer shaking with effort.

One day, Budig gently went through a resistance drill with Meyer, pushing down on his elbows—and he could feel Meyer stonewalling him with effort. He glanced at the coach's face and saw in Meyer's eyes a look he recognized from the hundreds of hours of practice he had watched. Anger. Meyer was fed up with Budig babying him through the rehab sessions. "You could see it—he didn't want me wasting his time," Budig recalled. "If he was going to be in there, he wanted to make the most of it." Budig pushed down harder on Meyer's elbows. Meyer didn't budge; Budig felt that Meyer was giving him maximum effort to make a point. *Okay,* Budig thought, *I'm beating you down, Old Man.* The rehab therapy that followed was much more intense.

For Budig, these sessions were a revelation. He had worked with Meyer for a decade, training the coach's players, getting up early and staying late, and yet he found he hardly knew him. Now, as they went through physical therapy together, Meyer asked Budig about his background, about Budig's wife and children, about his ambition. For the first time that Budig could remember, Meyer talked about himself.

They would work like this for months. After one session, Meyer handed Budig an envelope, which Budig opened after returning to his office. It contained five hundred dollars. Budig went back downstairs to Meyer's office. "Coach, I can't take this money," said Budig, explaining that it was his responsibility to do the sessions with Meyer—and besides, he said, he got much more out of their time together than Meyer would ever know.

Meyer started to cry. "I need to do this," he said. "Don't stop me from doing this."

Meyer reached over, hugged Budig, and kissed him on the cheek and told him he loved him. For Budig, the moment confirmed that Meyer was who Budig had always thought he was as a person.

CHAPTER 13

On the day before Meyer made coaching history, in the second week of January, 2009, he told a visitor that he had a place in mind for lunch where the prices were good. Plus, he explained chattily, he knew the owner, Mike Salem, and felt that Salem cared very much about his employees. And he spoke of Salem's father, Harold Salem, a pastor at Aberdeen's First Baptist Church, a man in his eighties who had a prolific collection of sermons—because he had never repeated a sermon and had saved them all.

"Park over there," Meyer said, pointing to a spot that was about one hundred feet removed from the door of the McDonald's.

The dunes of South Dakota's winter had formed in the parking lots throughout Aberdeen—the windblown berms of plowed snow piled between rows of cars. But Meyer, using his walker, didn't want to take the long way around; rather, he began climbing over an eighteen-inch berm, his body tilted precariously to the left as he balanced on the slope.

"We've got some snowshoes hanging in our garage," the visitor said. "I ought to send them to you."

"I only need one," Meyer replied, and then, because he was shaking with laughter at his own joke, he paused to settle his body before finishing his journey into the McDonald's.

After lunch, he had an errand to run, to a local jeweler to pick up his repaired wedding ring. The band had to be cut off in the hours after the accident because of the swelling in his left hand. As Meyer exited his van, he carefully planted his walker, making sure that the legs were stable amid the tiny rivers of ice that had formed in the jeweler's parking lot.

Philip Hutcheson had played for Meyer at David Lipscomb, and during a visit to his former coach in South Dakota after the accident, he thought: *What a brutal place to try to coach basketball.* Finding good players in such a sparsely populated area, was like trying to locate water holes in the desert, and there wasn't a natural lure to Aberdeen. UCLA boasted a beautiful, warm, and glamorous area. Duke players might be attracted by the program's renowned history and the school's excellent academic reputation. But if you coached in Aberdeen, Hutcheson knew, you were asking recruits to come to a small town of subzero winter temperatures, a place where the cold wind was constant and where the basketball team needed to practice at six A.M. For the coaches, most recruiting trips would be something in the range of three hundred miles each way.

And now Meyer's challenges had multiplied. Meyer had to

cope in this climate with a severe handicap; Hutcheson couldn't imagine trying to navigate with a walker or a wheelchair in a place where parking lots and driveways were often covered with ice and snow. He couldn't imagine a tougher place for Meyer to coach at this time than Northern State.

Meyer had gradually gained strength during the early portion of the Northern State schedule, as his body recovered from the accident. The Wolves had played a Thanksgiving tournament game when Meyer went to his assistant coach and told him at halftime that he had nothing left physically that day, and the assistant would have to run the team the rest of the game. But as the days passed, Meyer gained back some weight, and the color in his face returned, and Meyer and Randy Baruth talked about getting ready to assume their traditional roles; Meyer, by December, could get through all the practices and games. Northern State won eleven of their first thirteen games. On January 3, the Wolves defeated Upper Iowa, the 902nd victory of Meyer's career, matching Bob Knight's total. Their next scheduled game was set for January 10.

In the way that other coaches constantly reached out to Meyer, he would reach out to coaches he wanted to learn from. This is how he had befriended Vanderbilt baseball coach Tim Corbin. On a trip to Nashville to visit family, Meyer had gone to a Vanderbilt game, and in the fall of 2008, Corbin and Meyer settled on a date when Corbin could go to Aberdeen and see Northern State play: January 10.

After Northern State's January 3 victory, Corbin realized that the game he was scheduled to see could be the game in which Meyer would surpass Bob Knight's career mark for victories. Concerned about complicating Meyer's life on a day of extraordinary achievement, Corbin called Meyer to change the plans.

"Here's what you'll do," Meyer said evenly. "We'll pick you up at the airport, and you'll stay at our house." Meyer, the coach who had long taught his players to value process over product, didn't want Corbin to change his plans because of a statistic.

Northern State was to play the University of Mary that night, and Meyer informed Corbin that his seat for the game would be on the Wolves' bench—something he had done for other coaches and honored guests. When the Wolves had played their first game in the fall, Don Carda, the truck driver from the accident, had sat on the Northern State bench, along with his wife, Reva. This was something that Meyer did regularly, and of course he had no intention of treating this game, on this night, any differently from any other game. But to Corbin, it felt like an unbelievable gift to be able to be in this spot, on this day, listening to Meyer's pre-tip speech in which he implored his players to play the way they practiced.

Once the game started, Corbin watched Meyer in his wheelchair, his body tilted to the right, his eyes fixed on the players on the floor, his attention locked on the details. Six thousand four hundred and forty-four fans had filled Wachs Arena, and throughout the game, Corbin could feel their anxiety rise when the University of Mary put together scoring bursts cutting into Northern State's early lead, and could sense their exuberance every time a Northern State score moved Meyer closer to the record. Meyer might not have been focused on the record during the game, but the crowd was.

Northern State's Kevin Ratzsch drilled a three-point shot with four minutes and fifty-seven seconds remaining in the game, and with the Wolves' lead at seventeen points, those in the crowd began clapping, and chanting, "*Nine-Oh-Three . . . Nine-Oh-Three . . . Nine-Oh-Three.*"

Meyer remained stoic, and at the final buzzer, at the instant that Meyer had achieved more victories than any men's coach in

NCAA history, confetti streamed from the ceiling. Meyer's expression never changed as he rolled through the postgame handshakes with the University of Mary coaching staff and players. The fans stood and cheered and waited for some sort of ceremony to begin, and Meyer called the Wolves into a huddle in front of their bench.

Kyle Schwan wondered how his coach would acknowledge the 903rd victory, if at all. He had referred to it only one time in practice, angrily. "Screw records," he had said, imploring his players to focus on execution. Schwan wondered if his coach would finally bask just a little bit as he huddled with the players on the bench right after the game. But Schwan already knew the answer. "We're not here to celebrate this record," Meyer said. "We're here to get better as a team."

As the huddle broke up, Meyer turned his wheelchair out, the crowd roared, and players began slapping him on the shoulders. He looked into the stands and made eye contact with Carmen. All week, she hadn't been sure quite what to say. She understood her husband's need to stay focused on the moment at hand, and even hours before the game, she had been afraid to bring it up. But now he had 903 victories on his record. Smiling at her husband, Carmen raised her fists over her head. And Don Meyer smiled back.

A video began on the giant screen that hung on a wall, and the face of John Wooden appeared. "Congratulations, Don," said Wooden. "I don't know how you did it, but you did it."

Meyer laughed and rolled his wheelchair toward the scorer's table, where he was handed a microphone. Meyer stood on one leg. "We're never going to be able to thank all of you," he said. "But you need to know how much it means to us. And you need to keep praying for the leg to recover and the cancer maybe to go away. But most of all you need to pray that we all keep the spirit you all have exhibited toward our family and our team."

Don and Carmen Meyer at a Northern State ceremony a week after
Meyer achieved his 903rd career victory.

A week later, Northern State named the basketball court for him. Meyer's signature was painted in black in two-foot-high letters, on two corners of the wooden floor.

John Thune, one of South Dakota's U.S. senators, spoke at the ceremony. He had known Meyer for the better part of a decade, and he came from a basketball family—his father, Harold, had played at the University of Minnesota—and the senator had once attended a high school tournament with Meyer.

Thune had walked in a little late wearing a leather jacket, and sat next to Meyer. "What, did you ride in on a Harley?" Meyer asked flatly, never taking his eyes off the court. Thune had visited Meyer a couple of times in the hospital at Sioux Falls, and before the ceremony Thune went into the Wolves' locker room to hear Meyer's pregame talk with the players. Thune was struck by how intently the players listened and how Meyer commanded their attention.

After the game and ceremony, a half dozen of Meyer's former players went back to Meyer's house to hang out in his living room. After Meyer asked them for an honest assessment of what they had seen in the Northern State team, Meyer began reminiscing, telling the story from the mid-eighties of an ugly game that David Lipscomb had played, and Meyer chuckled about how the opposing coach had gone berserk during the game, inexplicably. Meyer was sure, with some pride, that he had gotten under the other coach's skin.

There was a silence, and then Hutcheson said, "Coach Meyer, I need to tell you what was really going on there." And with a twenty-year statute of limitations having expired, Hutcheson told him that the reason the other coach had reacted so crazily was that a player on the Lipscomb team had flipped his middle finger at him. Meyer was stunned by this revision of history.

"Well, crap," he said, grinning, "what other stories do we need to clean up?"

So for the next couple of hours, his ex-players drew the curtain and revised their shared history.

Hutcheson told Meyer for the first time about the events of a flight the team had taken for a national tournament game from Hutcheson's sophomore year. Meyer and his assistant coaches had driven to the tournament in Kansas City, and left Hutcheson—who, even at age twenty, already had the sensibility of a forty-five-year-old dad—to oversee the seventeen players and managers on their commercial flight from Nashville. When Hutcheson checked in the Lipscomb party at the ticket counter, he was surprised to get sixteen first-class tickets and one ticket for coach.

Hutcheson wasn't sure how to handle this before mentally drawing inspiration from the Bible, from Matthew 20:16: *The first shall be last, and the last shall be first.*

Hutcheson held up the seventeen tickets to his teammates, with the ticket for coach on the top. Hutcheson guessed that Al Cooper—a junior who had an elbows-out personality—would all but shove others out of the way to grab the first ticket. And this is exactly what happened. Cooper snatched the top ticket and, without looking at the seat assignment, he walked down the runway to the plane.

As the rest of the players began taking their seats in first class, Cooper watched them, smirking from the back of the plane, convinced that they were all playing a joke on him and that eventually they would get up and join him in coach. Then Darren Henrie, another sophomore, called over a flight attendant. "Please close the curtain so we can keep the riffraff out," Henrie said, and it was only as the drape closed that Cooper realized that first shall be last, and last shall be first.

Meyer and the players laughed at the old war stories, and at two A.M. they broke for some food that Carmen and Brooke had made, and a couple of the former players took off to drive to Omaha to catch a plane. But Tomlinson, Hutcheson, and former center Rob Browne stayed awake, lying on air mattresses on the floor at the feet of Meyer, who was in his leather chair. It wasn't until four thirty, after more storytelling, that Meyer began dozing.

Browne saw Carmen come out from the bedroom and reach down to touch Meyer's shoulder. He was half-asleep. "Don, it's time to go to bed," she said.

"No, no," he said. "I want to stay with my boys."

She pulled the blanket up around his shoulders, and he fell asleep.

CHAPTER 14

The Wolves lost in the playoffs, and Northern State concluded its tumultuous season with a 19–11 record. The assistant coaches had come to believe that the trials of the Wolves' season had eventually worn on the players, who had witnessed the near death of their coach before absorbing the news of his terminal illness, and then coped with the day-to-day uncertainty of his condition. Their season had ended in a haggard, disappointing defeat. But they had survived.

A few weeks later, Northern State assistant coach Randy Baruth, a thirty-two-year-old South Dakota native, drove over to Meyer's house before dawn to pick him up. Baruth had arranged a visit with Daniel Steffensen, a promising recruit who lived in

New Mexico, seventeen hours away. Baruth and Meyer intended to drive there, for there was no money for airfare, and at five A.M., Baruth turned Meyer's van westward. Meyer set a small stool on the floorboard of the car, placed pillows on top of the stool, and rested Little Buddy on top of the pillows.

Ten hours into the drive, Baruth closed in on Denver. "Do you want a break driving?" Meyer asked Baruth. His assistant said yes and pulled over in an empty lot at the Last Chance corners in Colorado, next to the four-way intersection of Highways 36 and 71. Meyer opened his car door and climbed out, balancing himself on his right foot and hopping around the front of the car, his hands splayed dramatically on the hood as he circled, like a suspected felon at a police roadblock. "Now I know what it's like to be frisked," he said, making his way to the driver's-side door.

Meyer had been able to get more sleep since the end of the season, and Baruth noticed that Meyer often arrived at the office later in the morning than he had in the past. He looked better, healthier, more rested. As Meyer climbed behind the wheel, however, Baruth noted that he was giddier than ever, almost playful.

Meyer moved the stool and pillows, re-set Little Buddy in a comfortable position, and adjusted the radio station to Rush Limbaugh's show. He was settled in and ready to go, and after a few miles, Meyer turned to Baruth and said, "Make sure you don't tell Carmen."

Baruth realized then that Meyer hadn't been cleared to drive by doctors or, more important, by Carmen. But Meyer was like a teenager taking the family car out for a spin. And anyway, Baruth really couldn't have stopped Meyer.

Randy Baruth was the youngest of five boys who had grown up on a South Dakota farm, and in the summer of 1999, he got a call from his oldest brother, Mick. "Hey, Don Meyer just took the Northern State job," Mick Baruth said.

"Who?" Randy Baruth responded. After he hung up the phone, he did an Internet search on Meyer and learned why his brother was so excited. The coaching successes, the popular videotapes, and the summer camps and clinics intrigued him.

Baruth had coached a girls' high school team in Parkston, South Dakota, for a couple of years, before landing a job with the men's program at North Dakota State University. Determined to learn as much as he could in the summer before he started at NDSU, Baruth worked at some summer camps and decided to go and watch Meyer's summer camps. On one of the days he was there, he went out to his car and happened to bump into Meyer. Baruth was intimidated as he introduced himself. "Oh, you're going to be at North Dakota State this year," Meyer said. "Come to my office—I've got a bunch of stuff for you."

Meyer gave him copies of all of his handouts, as he did with so many coaches. Later, as Baruth studied Northern State on tape, he knew he wanted to coach a team that smart and with that intensity.

Baruth decided that what he'd really like to do was work for Meyer in some capacity—and not long after that, the coaching dominoes fell his way. A spot opened up at Northern State, and Baruth walked away from the possibility of a $50,000 job on the staff at North Dakota State to take a $5,000-a-year support job working for Meyer. He stayed in one of the bedrooms in the Meyers' basement for three months, and one night after midnight, the door to his room opened. Baruth, dead asleep, was startled and jumped to his feet, thinking he might be the victim of a robbery. "Hey, it's okay," a voice said from the doorway. "It's Coach." And Meyer offered Baruth the job of assistant coach, because another assistant had just taken a job elsewhere.

Baruth and Meyer clicked immediately. Like other assistant coaches who had worked for Meyer in years past, Baruth felt that Meyer included him in the decision-making process, listened to his suggestions, and taught him. A student coach had once re-marked to Baruth that in Meyer's program, every person doing every job was essential, whether you were preparing a tray of food for the players at a meal or you were an assistant coach working with the guards on transition defense. No job within the North-ern State program was any less important or any more important than any other. Meyer would react as strongly when a player mis-treated a manager as he did to malfeasance on the court.

When Meyer disagreed with something that Baruth was doing—maybe in recruiting, or in the coaching of the program's forwards and centers—the older man would say, *Randy, I under-stand your perspective on this and see what you're doing. Let's look at it from another perspective and see what you think.* Only twice did Meyer snap at Baruth in the first five years they worked together. Meyer assigned his assistant coaches the responsibility of mak-ing substitutions during games; this way, they could closely monitor the fatigue of the players on the court and the foul situ-ations, leaving Meyer to focus on the players' adjustments. Dur-ing one game in Baruth's first season with the team, Matt Hammer—then one of Northern State's best players—was on the bench early in the second half with three fouls. Meyer turned and asked Baruth, "When are we getting Matt back in there?" Two more possessions followed, and Hammer was still on the bench. Meyer again turned and asked, "When are we getting Matt back in there?"

Baruth defended himself—"He's already got three fouls"—in a tone that he knew immediately was not appropriate for the situ-ation. Meyer barked, "Hey, if you want your own coaching job, go and get it. Get his butt back into the game."

A few days later, Baruth and Meyer met, and Baruth apolo-gized for what he had said. Meyer explained evenly that, through his experience, he had learned there were times the team's needs were such that you had to risk putting a player on the court despite his foul trouble. Both put the incident behind them; there was never a moment, Baruth felt, when he had been unfairly squashed by Meyer. "There was never a feeling of 'I'm the head coach and you're the assistant coach, and don't you forget it,' " said Baruth. He felt necessary. He felt that Meyer cared about him.

The two men worked well together, coaching together, traveling together, talking about basketball and life. Randy and his wife, Meghan, would come to view Don and Carmen Meyer as the most influential people in their lives other than their parents.

After the accident, Meyer trusted Baruth with the basketball program that he loved. He trusted Baruth to do what he could not do on a given day, to generate energy or instruction, to discipline the players when necessary. Besides Carmen, Baruth probably had the most intimate knowledge of Meyer's medical situation. Baruth was there to help, and the friendship between the men grew.

Like family, Don Meyer and Baruth had a personal history, like two people who'd gone through college together. Whenever their long recruiting drives took them to North Dakota, they made a point of stopping at the Bismarck restaurant called The China Star, where Meyer would dig into the buffet—at about ten dollars a pop—and then immediately fall asleep in the car, with Baruth at the wheel. One day, Baruth was stopped for speeding by a North Dakota state trooper on the way to see a recruit, and when a truck nearly sideswiped the trooper, he gave a quick warning and went off in pursuit of the truck—and, incredibly, as Baruth drove home, the same trooper stopped him for speeding again. "Golly, Coach, what are you doing?" the trooper asked Baruth, as Meyer shook with laughter in the passenger seat. When Baruth explained about their long recruiting trips, and

Randy Baruth (in dark shirt) and Don Meyer.

how they had to be at practice at six A.M., the trooper let him off with a warning again.

Meyer preferred to time his portion of the drives with Baruth so that he could listen to Colin Cowherd of ESPN or Limbaugh—and he listened to Limbaugh even when he wasn't driving. Baruth would glance over and see that Meyer was asleep and turn the dial to some other programming—and Meyer would wake. It was as if Limbaugh's voice was soothing for him, Baruth decided.

The recruiting visit with the Steffensen family in New Mexico went well, they thought at the time (although in the end, the player did not sign with Northern). A little before noon, Meyer and Baruth headed back to Aberdeen, with Meyer at the wheel for a stretch, before switching places just after the two reached the South Dakota border. The two friends pulled into Aberdeen at four o'clock in the morning, and Baruth helped Meyer move his stuff from the car into the house and then left.

Baruth thought Meyer was the most driven person he had ever met. In years past, when Meyer got home from a recruiting trip this late, he might sleep for a few hours but still be at the office by eight A.M. But on this day, Meyer didn't come in until early in the afternoon, and after a couple of hours he went home. In the aftermath of the thirty-four hours of driving to New Mexico, the thought occurred to Baruth for the first time that Meyer might never be able to will his way back to working eighteen-hour days.

Meyer always told Baruth and his other assistants to make sure that they let him know when they pursued a job they wanted, because he wanted to be able to help them as much as possible. As Northern's season began drawing to a close, Meyer repeated that line to Baruth—and Baruth felt that there was more weight behind the words. In March, Meyer heard about a head coaching job in Nebraska and mentioned it to Baruth, adding that he knew the athletic director at the school and might have some influence. Baruth had no intention of chasing other positions; he wasn't really interested, considering Meyer's physical fragility.

A job opened on the staff of Colorado State, which Meyer encouraged Baruth to consider. Meghan Baruth returned from the recruiting weekend at the school excited about the move, because it would mean more time for the Baruths to be together in their young marriage; she was in the process of finishing off her Ph.D. in exercise science at the University of South Carolina, and had a better chance of finding work in that field in Colorado than in South Dakota. Randy Baruth wasn't so sure, initially; he was rooted in the Northern State program and he felt a strong allegiance to Meyer. He wanted to do right by Meyer, and it was deeply important to him to know that Meyer felt he was making the right choice. Meyer asked the Baruths to come to their house to talk about the job.

Sitting in his living room, Meyer looked at Baruth and said, "It's time, Randy. It's time for you to go."

Months later, as Baruth reflected on their conversation, it became clear to him what had taken place: Meyer knew that he might not be able to coach much longer, and he did not want Baruth left suddenly without a job, and without having taken the next step in coaching. And Meyer knew that unless he had pushed his assistant gently out of the Northern State gym, Baruth would not leave.

While Baruth had wanted to be sure to do all he could to help Meyer, his friend and mentor with a terminal illness, Meyer had been looking out for Baruth all along as well.

On the day that Baruth left Aberdeen, he went by the gym and said good-bye to each of the players individually, knowing that if he tried to speak to them together, he would break down. Then he found Meyer in his wheelchair. Baruth put his arm around the coach. "There will be no hugs here," Meyer said. "No sentimental crap here. I'll be out to visit you soon, and we'll be talking."

Baruth understood Meyer enough to know that his friend didn't like hellos or good-byes. It wasn't long after he left that Meyer called him on the phone, repeatedly, and Baruth noticed over time that the coach spoke to him as if he had never left. Meyer constantly said "we" when referring to the program, and also when referring to Baruth. And Baruth realized he shared in something that lasted: Like Meyer's generations of players, he shared in a legacy.

CHAPTER 15

A couple of weeks after Meyer's road trip to New Mexico, in April of 2009, he stood at a podium on the campus of Lipscomb University and spoke to about eight hundred students. Philip Hutcheson sat near Meyer and watched the faces of those sitting in the first rows. Hutcheson was struck by their response to his old coach; they seemed to be completely invested in what Meyer was saying.

As a fifth grader, Hutcheson had attended Meyer's first summer basketball camp and had gone on to play for Meyer and become the all-time leading scorer in college basketball history. Hutcheson had heard Meyer speak countless times, in team meetings and in practices and in chapel, and he knew by heart the coach's sermons on excellence. But he had taken the words for granted, he thought, as he watched another generation of students focused so intently on Meyer's mantras.

This was just one part of a special day, a reunion that had seemed unthinkable, given the ugly background of Meyer's departure from Lipscomb in 1999, after a twenty-four-year tenure.

The school had been part of the National Association of Intercollegiate Athletics, a second tier of college programs separate from the NCAA's Division I. The NAIA had produced basketball players like Dennis Rodman and Scottie Pippen. But in the late nineties, the administration of Lipscomb began considering a move to Division I—a switch that Meyer vehemently opposed.

He believed that the university would have extraordinary difficulty raising the funds needed year after year to meet the costs of travel as well as the expense of adding the sports programs required to join a new conference. He felt, too, that Lipscomb—a church-affiliated school squeezed among the University of Tennessee, Vanderbilt, and other Division I programs in the state of Tennessee—would have difficulty luring the level of student athletes needed to have a strong program. Lipscomb contended annually for NAIA championships, but at Division I, Meyer believed, the team might have trouble continuing that tradition. He felt that Lipscomb should have more appreciation for the strong programs it already had.

Lipscomb administrators formed a committee to discuss the idea of moving to Division I. At one gathering, Meyer listened for a few minutes and then cut in. "I told myself when I came here I wasn't going to talk," Meyer said, "but I just can't say nothing anymore. I think we are absolutely crazy if we do this."

As the tensions between Meyer and the school's administration worsened, a high-ranking executive at Lipscomb said to the coach, "Maybe you're just not willing to put in the work that's required to win in Division I." For Meyer, this was akin to questioning his integrity.

Meyer was under the impression that there would be more talk about remaining in the NAIA, but he had learned that a decision had already been made. Feeling completely misled, Don Meyer, one of the most accomplished basketball coaches in the country, wrote out his resignation—and angrily dropped it into campus mail.

A few weeks later—and a few months before he applied for the job at Northern State—he made a forty-five-minute video meant for those who had been part of his program. With a microphone attached to his shirt, he led a cameraman on a tour of McQuiddy Gymnasium, where the Bisons had played, the team room, and different areas of the campus where the summer basketball camps had been staged. For most of the tape, Meyer told stories and cracked jokes and aimed playful words at different players.

At the end of the videotape, Meyer sat at a desk with a yellow pad of notes in front of him and spoke directly into the camera. "Hopefully, I'll be working next year," Meyer said, "and if you guys are driving down the road and you happened to see a Captain D's, you might want to look and see if I'm there. If they don't take coupons, then I'm probably not going to be in there." Meyer paused for a moment and pursed his lips; it was evident that he was fighting his emotions. "You know, when I know where I am [coaching], and you know where I am, I'd be the proudest guy in the world to show you off to our guys who are playing for me and say that you were a guy who played for us at Lipscomb. You guys don't know the pride people have for you in this program."

Meyer mentioned, with the video camera rolling, that Bob Knight had been a poor defensive player in college, and as a coach he had emphasized defense. "I always emphasized team," Meyer went on, "because I'm probably the most selfish person in the world. But being around you guys, and you were trying to help each other, it sort of made me be a better person. And I hope you have that kind of attitude and you'll try to foster that idea of giving. The only way you're ever going to win is by giving. Nobody ever wins anything by taking and using people and tromping on them. You have to try to bring people up and build them up; you have to give.

"I felt like with the kind of kids we had, even when we lost, we won."

At the end of the tape, he encouraged his former players to support Lipscomb athletics. But for a lot of the people who had been part of the program, the fact that the university had allowed a split with Meyer to happen was unforgivable. (In a terrible coincidence, the announcement that the school was shifting to Division I happened to fall on the exact same day that Wade Tomlinson's son drowned, which seemed to exacerbate the hurt feelings.)

Meyer's departure from Lipscomb meant that others who worked in his program had to make choices too. Barb Anderson had worked at Lipscomb for twenty-two years, the last seventeen of those as Meyer's assistant. Continuing to work for the university after he left was almost unthinkable. Meyer had always included her in the decisions made within the program, kept his office door open, and supported her resolutely through personal trouble; she would come to think of Meyer as the best friend she had, other than her husband. And she felt that the program, under Meyer's leadership, had accomplished something important, because the kids left Lipscomb as good people—great young adults. "I know that some of the kids who came through the program would have been fine even if they didn't play for Coach," Anderson recalled. "But he made such a difference in so many lives, and I was blessed to be a part of it. . . . To me, he represented everything that Lipscomb stood for, and they just kicked him in the teeth."

So Barb Anderson, believing that the program would never be anything close to what it had been under Meyer, quit her job. For years, bitterness lingered over Meyer's departure—in Meyer and in many of his former players, who simply declined to support the school. Long after Meyer left the program under such objectionable circumstances, a student called Wade Tomlinson to solicit a donation on behalf of Lipscomb. Tomlinson's denial was polite and firm, and he told the student: *You go tell the president that I'm not giving money, and here's why: It's because of the way it ended with Don Meyer.*

It was due to this history of anger and hurt feelings between the Meyer clan of players and Lipscomb University that Philip Hutcheson had gone to visit Meyer in the hospital in Sioux Falls with some concern. Hutcheson was going to see the coach because of his personal connection, but he also had some news: Hutcheson was thinking about taking the job as athletic director at Lipscomb University, and he wasn't quite sure how his old coach would react. Hutcheson loved Meyer and deeply appreciated what Meyer had given him as a coach, but he also loved his alma mater.

Meyer could barely speak when Hutcheson arrived at the hospital in Sioux Falls, but when Hutcheson told him about how he had a shot to take the job, Meyer seemed to perk up, and his response was unequivocal: Hutcheson should work for Lipscomb.

And Meyer immediately started offering advice on how he should handle the job. Hutcheson slept in a chair next to Meyer that night, and from time to time Meyer, under heavy medication, would stir awake and say, in a soft but gravelly voice, "Hutch . . . you got a piece of paper? Take this down." He would offer another new thought, and Hutcheson, who had written

Meyer and his former players at Lipscomb University, April 28, 2009.

down so many of Meyer's words in notebooks as a camper and a player, dutifully jotted down his advice.

"You know, Hutch," Meyer said at one point, "I thought I was right. And they thought they were right. And I guess sometimes you can both be sort of right."

He was talking about Lipscomb University.

"Hutch, if you decide to do this, and you need me to help," Meyer said, "then you just let me know."

And so, weeks later, the new athletic director for Lipscomb University, Philip Hutcheson, scheduled a fund-raiser for April 28, 2009. The guest speaker: Don Meyer. The event was called The First Annual Don Meyer Evening of Excellence.

Meyer spent the morning on the Lipscomb campus, speaking to the students at chapel, before a lunch meeting with the university's coaches. Captain D's was brought in for lunch, in Meyer's honor. In the first part of the night program, Meyer and Hutcheson sat together on a stage, each with a microphone. Meyer's left leg was propped up on his chair. Meyer grinned as they started and looked at his ex-center, who had not been particularly fleet in college. "I never thought I'd see the day, Hutch, that you'd be faster than me," Meyer jabbed, and the crowd laughed. "Little Buddy just can't make it."

Meyer and Hutcheson talked together casually for about half an hour; later, Meyer spoke for the better part of an hour from a dais. But as Hutcheson watched, he sensed that what everybody wanted that night was a chance to visit, like at a college reunion. So many of Meyer's former players came back for the event that in the days that followed, Hutcheson kept hearing about different players from different generations of Lipscomb teams who had shown up. Barb Anderson wrote down as many names as she could of those who had been there—from Ricky Bowers to Darren Henrie to Mark Campbell to Wade Tomlinson, and so many others—and her final unofficial count was seventy.

Barb Anderson never would have come back, she was sure, if she hadn't known that Meyer would approve. But she saw how proud he was, how happy, and for her "it felt like Christmas. It felt like the whole family was back together again."

The players felt a deep connection, because they had experienced something special together. They wanted to visit with Meyer, with one another. Some players who had returned to campus for this night hadn't been at Lipscomb in years. It felt like a homecoming, Hutcheson thought.

Meyer remained in a reception room for a time, greeting and catching up with old friends. But he specifically asked Hutcheson to arrange a separate meeting with those who had been part of his basketball program. It was after ten o'clock at night when Meyer and dozens of ex-players gathered around him inside what was left of the gym where they had played and he had coached. Somebody wanted to take a picture of the old group, and they gathered around Meyer, who was sitting in a chair at first. But Meyer wanted to stand for the shots.

With all the pictures taken, there was a pause, and Meyer told the players to huddle together. Meyer was wearing a blue sport coat, and as he began to talk, Browne noticed that his old coach had goose bumps on his neck.

"All of that stuff about [Lipscomb] going Division I," Meyer said, "that's all a bunch a crap. So forget it.

"Lipscomb is trying to do the right thing," he told the players, "and we all need to get behind Philip and help him any way we can."

One of Meyer's simple rules as coach was that he wanted his players to be ready with their hands, always. Ready to catch a pass. Ready to catch and shoot. So he insisted that throughout practice they keep their hands up, in front of their chests, in the ready position.

As Meyer spoke to his former players—some of them in their fifties and most of them fathers—Rob Browne, realized that he had drawn his own hands up to his chest. Browne glanced around the group of ex-players—Hutcheson, Tomlinson, others—and they had their hands up too.

Brooke Napier sat at a nearby table watching her father with deep relief and pleasure. He had given so much to the school. "When the ties were cut, it was painful," she said. "It was difficult to see him hurting, to see everything he had worked so hard to build gone, and it was painful to see the bitterness and pain continue to fester over the years. But after the wreck, Dad's bitterness lifted." It was healing not only for him but for all of the Meyers.

He finished his talk with his players, but they all lingered, very late, until about one A.M. When Carmen Meyer came back to the gym to retrieve him, Don Meyer was asleep in his wheelchair.

CHAPTER 16

On the night that Meyer surpassed Knight's record, Tom and Cathie Anderson of Sturgis, South Dakota, got a text message from their youngest son: *HE DID IT!* Casey Anderson wrote from the gym at Northern State University, where he had played for Meyer for three seasons. The words and the sentence structure were apropos for Anderson, in their energy, their passion.

Four months later, just after midnight on May 7, Casey Anderson left the apartment of some friends and returned to his own place. He typed out a text message to his parents, to some friends, and his former girlfriend:

Mom, Dad, I'm sorry. I'm just not cut out for this place.
I love you guys so much. I'm not scared. This is for the best.

Not long after that, Aberdeen police kicked in the door of Casey Anderson's apartment and found him; he had hanged himself. Casey Donald Anderson, twenty-two years old, had a faint pulse, but he could not be revived.

Randy Baruth, still in his last weeks with the Northern State program, called Meyer at four A.M. "Casey's gone," Baruth said.

"He did not," Meyer said.

"Yes," Baruth said. "He's gone."

When Casey Anderson had played for Meyer, he and the other players were asked to jot down their resting heart rate when they checked into Meyer's office. For most, that meant writing down a number in the fifties or sixties. Casey's resting heart rate was usually eighty-five to ninety, a reflection, teammates thought, of his personality.

Casey had always been outgoing, sociable, with an enormous smile. When he was a young child, he liked to wear suits and carry the family backgammon case to school as if he was taking a briefcase to work. One Easter, he dressed in a suit with a black bow tie and mentioned to his parents with some distaste that there were actually kids at church who hadn't bothered to get dressed up—believing, of course, that those plastic spurs that he had worn on his cowboy boots were well within the bounds of good taste.

When Casey was in high school, he was a last-second fill-in to play a comedian at a school assembly after another kid had called in sick, and he had improvised his act and performed so well—without telling his parents about it—that for days others sought out Tom and Cathie Anderson to tell them how funny Casey had been.

But mostly Casey Anderson loved basketball. Tom Anderson and his son would go to a local gym and take five hundred shots a night, and when he was a sophomore, he had a growth spurt of some six inches, eventually reaching six foot seven. As the teenager grew into his body, Casey played football and ran track, and he became a formidable basketball player, with eye-catching, angular athleticism. In the summer after his junior year, Anderson played for the South Dakota team in a basketball tournament in Las Vegas, where college coaches watched them play from the sidelines. That day, Bobby Knight happened to be sitting between Don Meyer and his assistant coach, Randy Baruth. "Who out on the floor do you think we should recruit?" Meyer asked Knight.

Knight pointed at number 45, a kid with long arms wearing a dark blue jersey. Casey Anderson. "I'd recruit that long, lanky kid," said Knight.

And so Meyer recruited Anderson, and in a sense, Anderson recruited Northern State: He came back from a visit and told his parents how much he loved the place, how seriously they took basketball there. "This is the place for me," Anderson told his mother and father. He didn't bother looking at other schools before committing to Northern, and to Meyer.

That was about the time the soreness in his left foot began to take hold of him.

The first thought was that maybe Anderson had hurt his ankle in some way, but the pain worsened during his senior year in high school. The diagnosis shifted, and the source of the problem was thought to be the navicular bone, in the arch of the foot. Meyer arranged for surgery to be done on Anderson in Nashville, and as he tended to do, he called Brooke to inform her that Casey Anderson and a graduate assistant were going to stay at her house.

Brooke's four sons immediately gravitated to Anderson, in a way that all children tended to. When Northern State held basketball clinics for kids, children seemed to hang on him three or four at a time. Brett Newton, who would become one of Anderson's closest friends on the team, thought Casey had a gift for working with kids; Newton had never seen anything like it.

What Anderson wanted was to be a great basketball player; he had Meyer's passion for the sport and it created a tight bond. Once, when Anderson and Meyer were out at a restaurant together, Anderson walked up behind Meyer's bald head, blew on it the way you would a pane of glass, and then mockingly shined it with his elbow. Other players on the team couldn't imagine anyone even attempting something like that. Meyer just laughed. Tom and Cathie felt he was the right coach for their son.

But Casey Anderson could not get what he wanted most. His foot pain persisted, even after his surgery. Anderson redshirted his first season, played in just sixteen games in his first year, then one game in his second year of eligibility. For topical, temporary relief, he began to use Lidocaine patches on his foot. Patients are advised to wear one for no more than twelve hours, but Anderson, in his effort to relieve his pain, wore two at a time the whole day. He was desperate, and Meyer feared that Anderson's own self-worth was depending solely on his ability to play basketball.

Anderson was strong and fast. On the first sprint of the day, Anderson would beat his teammates down the court, displaying all the parts needed for a great basketball player. But on the second sprint, he would sometimes finish last, and Meyer could see Anderson's pain in the way he ran, and with sadness, he would tell his assistants to get Anderson off the court for his own good. "I hurt every time he jumps," Meyer told them. "I hurt every time he comes down." Unable to run pain-free, Anderson started lifting weights relentlessly.

The fact that Anderson couldn't be good at basketball, Brett Newton felt, "just tore him down." During Anderson's third year at Northern State, he talked to Brett Newton about getting some beer, and joked about using his fake ID, which had a picture of Anderson when he was very young. Newton laughed at the suggestion; of course, he would get caught. Anderson tried it anyway, stopping at a liquor store in Aberdeen where you could buy beer in a drive-through.

The clerk looked at Anderson's ID, looked up, and said, "Shut off your car." She was calling the police. Newton was petrified about what might happen to them. Anderson looked over at him and told him to take off, so Newton ran back to his dorm room.

When the police arrived, Anderson informed them that it had been his intention to drink the beer and then kill himself. Anderson was taken to a hospital, where Meyer and Baruth came to see him. They spoke to him about how much he was loved, the unique gifts that he had to connect with children. That night, Anderson tried to hang himself in the shower, unsuccessfully.

Casey's favorite cookie was oatmeal raisin, so Meyer's daughter Brooke sent along some cookies to the hospital, with a card from her sons. Anderson sent a thank-you note, including a picture of a puppy he and his girlfriend had found. He had autographed a basketball for the boys, too, and Brooke Napier was worried by the words he had written:

I hope you guys are behaving, I miss you. . . . Keep a positive outlook, because life could always be worse. Casey Anderson, #20

Anderson had played in only seventeen games in his first three years at Northern State, and it became clear to the coaching staff that he would probably no longer be able to contribute as a player. Knowing how it would gnaw at him, Meyer and Baruth drove to Sturgis to talk with Tom and Cathie Anderson about their son.

Meyer explained that Northern State was limited to ten scholarships and that in Anderson's three seasons on scholarship, he had barely played because of his injuries. Meyer told the Andersons that, going forward, Casey would no longer attend Northern on one of the basketball scholarships—but what Meyer would do was to raise money to cover Anderson's tuition and board so that he could finish his degree at Northern State. The Andersons listened and accepted this, but as the coaches left, Meyer felt awful, torn between the realities of trying to run a college basketball program and the emotional needs of a fragile young man. "I feel like an Army officer assigned to go to a home to inform them about the passing of a loved one," Meyer said to Baruth.

He had wanted to tell the Andersons before he spoke with their son, out of concern about how he would react—and Casey Anderson was devastated. He tearfully called his parents, and they were ready to jump into the car and drive to Aberdeen. "I think he's going to be okay," Anderson's girlfriend assured them, but the days that followed were frightening for Tom and Cathie Anderson. Their son was, on one hand, so empathetic, so in touch with the feelings of others; on the other hand, he seemed unreachable, his sadness beyond reassurance. "When he couldn't play basketball," said Tom Anderson, "he couldn't understand why."

Casey Anderson transferred to Black Hills State University, near home, intending to play basketball, but then returned to Northern State after just one semester to finish school. When ESPN aired video from the night Meyer broke the record for most coaching victories, Cathie and Tom Anderson could see their son in the background.

In early May, Anderson's feet felt good, and he had played two-on-two and three-on-three at the Northern State court with Newton. Newton would recall that Anderson had dominated, jumping all over the place, dunking, scoring, doing everything he had wanted to do. And at about six o'clock in the morning on May 7, Newton got a call from Baruth telling him that Anderson was dead.

Brett Newton drove to the memorial service with his own mother, the two of them talking during the drive about what had happened to his friend, trying to understand. He had had so many gifts, Brett Newton told his mother, but he just hadn't seen them in himself. "Why was someone so gifted not happy with himself?" he asked.

The First Presbyterian Church in Sturgis, South Dakota, overflowed for Anderson's service. After Reverend Denzel Nonhof opened with a recounting of the basic facts of Anderson's life, a song that the young man had listened to, "Second Chance" by Shinedown, was played over the church sound system, with its chorus:

Tell my mother, tell my father I've done the best I can
To make them realize this is my life, I hope they understand

Meyer got up to speak. He had prepared himself for this, and thought he could get through it without crying. But as he looked over at the casket and saw Casey Anderson wearing a Northern State basketball jacket, his voice cracked.

"You don't like to have favorite players, but he was one of my favorites," Meyer said. "He was just like a young colt, running around and jumping. So much energy."

Meyer told the story of how Bob Knight had told him to recruit Casey, and about the first recruiting visit to the Andersons' home. "I remember the home visit," Meyer said. "First of all, we tried to find the home. That was pretty tough."

Others in the church chuckled. "Those people didn't want to be bothered," Meyer said. "I think it's easier to find hell than to find that place.

"We sat out on that screened-in porch area . . . with a dog. A woodstove. My wife won't let me have a dog. . . . It was a great, great house," said Meyer. "A great home. Great family.

"We had good food. I always remember that from our home visits. If we got bad food, we'd just drop the kid from our recruiting."

There was laughter.

Meyer talked about Anderson helping to run Northern State's summer basketball camps, about his connection with children, about how he had swept up a mentally handicapped boy named Jake in his arms. "He was a magnet for little kids," said Meyer. "Casey would carry them all over.

"Now he's got a heavenly body," he continued. "It's better than his earth body. It doesn't have stress fractures. It doesn't have a torn-up shoulder. He's probably in the weight room up there, lifting. He's getting the key from God so he can lift all he can."

Casey Anderson was an organ donor, Meyer noted. And when Brooke, his daughter, told her sons that their friend Casey had died, she had mentioned this to them. "Momma, is Casey's heart still beating?" Zev had asked. "Yes, Zev, it's still beating in somebody else's chest, for somebody else."

Meyer's voice quavered. "It always says in the Bible, 'Unless you have the spirit and the heart of a little child, you'll never enter heaven,' " he said. "Now, I know Casey had that heart of a little child. He loved kids. He wanted to be around kids.

"I believe Casey's at peace. I believe that. . . . I know Casey's at peace, in God's arms."

It was snowing outside when Casey Anderson was taken for burial; the wind was blowing on a hillside cemetery. It was one of the coldest days that Meyer could ever remember.

When Tom and Cathie Anderson went to clean out Casey Anderson's apartment, they found a collection of notes that he had gotten from parents for his work in the summer camp, and stacks of letters he had gotten from kids. On his bulletin board was the artwork from Meyer's grandsons that had come with the package of oatmeal raisin cookies, meant to cheer him up.

*Casey Anderson (right) with teammate Kevin Ratzsch
and four Meyer grandchildren.*

CHAPTER 17

In early June of 2009, Meyer received word that he would be honored at the ESPYs as the winner of the Jimmy V. Award for Perseverance. He was philosophically opposed to the concept of spending money on clothes, but when Carmen raised the idea of getting a suit for the ESPYs ceremony, to be held in the Nokia Theatre in Los Angeles, he agreed without griping.

He had worn sport jackets throughout most of his adult life but did not own a suit, other than a leisure suit he had purchased in the seventies. So Carmen and Don went to Herberger's, a regional department store in Aberdeen's Lakewood Mall. With the help of a couple of folks there, they picked out a black suit with small pinstripes, a tie, and black shoes. Because of Meyer's long arms, however, they could not find a shirt in the store that would fit him. His daughter Brooke was commissioned to find a shirt at a store in Nashville, and she sent it along to Aberdeen.

The Meyers were flown first-class to Los Angeles, and after they checked into their room at the Millennium Biltmore, they were given a stuffed gift bag, the contents of which the Meyer offspring found amazing: a watch, an audio system, a specialized showerhead, and other stuff. Don Meyer was less than excited when he saw how much he would have to pay in taxes if he accepted it. Nonetheless, in the spirit of the trip, he absorbed the price of the gift bag.

On the Meyers' first full day in California, he and his entourage climbed into a van headed for Encino to visit John Wooden. Years before, Wooden had met Meyer and felt a bond with him over their love of basketball, because they had both grown up on midwestern farms. "We're both country boys," Wooden had recalled in the spring of 2009. "I had a good feel for him even before I met him." Wooden had gone to Aberdeen to speak at Meyer's summer camp, and after he finished, a long line of campers and coaches formed to get Wooden's autograph. Meyer tried to step in after a while, to relieve Wooden of the burden of signing all the basketballs and photos and slips of paper, but Wooden insisted on staying and got through every request.

After Meyer's party arrived in Encino, he pushed on the intercom button to call Wooden. "Yeah, hi, Coach, we're here to talk about black and white cows," he said, pulling on the thread of a running joke between the two men.

Wooden hosted his guests from a wheelchair in his living room wearing a UCLA-blue light sweater. When Wooden saw Meyer, he grinned impishly and said, "Don! What happened to your hair?"

The two men laughed, and then they began to tell the stories

John Wooden and Don Meyer visit at Wooden's apartment.

that old friends tell, repeating their favorite shared jokes. Wooden talked about his father, Joshua Wooden, who he said had never raised his voice and had always been gentle with animals. He recalled once how a teamster had been rough with some horses, and his father had gone over and asked if he could hold the reins; after he spoke to the horses, the animals immediately responded to him, becoming calm. Wooden talked about how he thought mules were much smarter than horses and more apt to learn when you wanted them to make a turn in a field.

In the foyer of Wooden's apartment, a small bookcase was filled entirely with books about Abraham Lincoln, and Wooden talked about how a short time of Lincoln's boyhood was spent in Indiana. Wooden talked about baseball, about how much he admired Angels Manager Mike Scioscia. Wooden then told the story of how he had met his late wife, Nell: He had been plowing a field and saw her and two friends stopped alongside to watch—and he initially thought she was laughing at him. From that initial skirmish a fifty-three-year marriage was launched.

Wooden glanced over at Carter, Meyer's fifteen-year-old granddaughter, who had been silent for more than an hour as she listened. "Did you say something?" Wooden asked abruptly, and she smiled. In this way he began to draw her into the conversation, and whenever she retreated in the last hour of the visit, he'd smile and say again to her: "You say something?"

Wooden sat cheerily for pictures. Meyer pushed himself up with his walker and hopped over to the side of Wooden's wheelchair, where the two men posed. They thanked each other with a hug, and Wooden handed Meyer a small laminated card.

As the Meyer entourage headed back to the Millennium, Meyer sat in the front passenger seat of the van and just grinned. "How about that?" Meyer said. "He's unbelievable."

————

He wrote out a draft of his speech the next afternoon, and after putting on his new suit, with the left pant leg pinned up underneath Little Buddy, he stuffed the speech into his front pocket.

The red carpet in front of the Nokia Theatre included Kobe Bryant, Serena Williams, Michael Phelps, the U.S. men's soccer team, Arizona quarterback Kurt Warner, Danica Patrick, Olympic gymnast Nastia Liukin, Terrell Owens, Lisa Leslie—and the featured speaker of the night, Don Meyer, who was brought to his front-row seats with Carmen. The parade of stars continued to pass by, with other famous athletes and their husbands and wives and dates all filing in fashionably late. There were eight thousand folks in the building, wearing custom-made suits and glittering dresses, and the many diamonds sparkled in the lights. Meyer was astounded. "Can you imagine how much money was spent on clothes?" he marveled under his breath.

Samuel L. Jackson was the host, and at the outset of the show—which was being taped, to be shown four days later—there was a problem with the TelePrompTer. Meyer suddenly became concerned about whether he should have given a copy of his speech to someone to be loaded into the TelePrompTer and whether he would be able to see the TelePrompTer from the stage. And as the awards were passed out for the best performances of the year, the acceptance speeches of the recipients tended to last one or two sentences; Meyer's speech, as written, would probably require five minutes or so. During a break in the show, Meyer pulled out the yellow notepad paper and a pen and prepared to rewrite.

"Do you think I should cut some stuff out?" he asked Carmen.

"I think your award is a little different than a lot of the others," she assured him.

At the next break, a show producer came to escort Don Meyer behind the curtain to prepare for his segment. Jerry Meyer, sitting some twenty rows behind, saw this and followed him, and sitting on a couch together, they went over the speech one last time.

The son looked over his father's words and offered some thoughts and a lot of encouragement. *Yes, yes, this is going to work. . . . Yeah, that line is going to be great.* In this moment, Jerry Meyer was the coach. Don Meyer looked at his son and was touched—by his son's intellect, his understanding of words, and his ability to rise to the moment. This was Jerry in his element, his father thought.

But mostly he was touched by Jerry's gesture. Don Meyer knew that Jerry simply wanted to make sure that his father was in the right frame of mind, and provided with the proper dose of emotional support if some was needed, before he went onstage. The father nodded and listened to the son he admired.

The break ended, and onstage, ESPN's Chris Berman introduced the Jimmy V. Award, explaining its genesis. Just out of sight behind a curtain, Meyer stood next to actor Rob Lowe, and the two men chatted. "Don't upstage me, Coach," Lowe told him, kiddingly. "This is my world." But the more they talked, the more Lowe could see how comfortable Meyer was, and the more he thought Meyer's words would be the highlight of the night.

Lowe introduced a video piece about Meyer's accident and cancer diagnosis, and at the end of it, the crowd inside the Nokia Theatre rose and clapped and clapped as Meyer pushed his way out on his walker, moving slowly to the podium. As the cheering continued, Meyer lifted his right hand slightly to acknowledge the reception. Meyer pulled out his glasses and propped them on the bridge of his nose, and as the cheering stilled, he unfolded the yellow sheets of notepad paper

"We don't have any TelePrompTers in South Dakota," he began drolly, "so I'm just going to read this, if that's okay. . . ."

There was laughter.

He thanked the show's organizers, and then said, "I'm just a small college coach from Northern State University in Aberdeen, South Dakota. That means when I leave the motel tomorrow morning at four fifteen, I'll take all the soap, shampoo . . ."

The crowd laughed with him and threatened to drown out his punch line, so he paused. The audience was with him. "And even the shower cap," he said, staring out from his bald head.

Lowe looked out into the audience and saw Kobe Bryant turn to his wife and laugh; others were doing the same. To see all of these world-famous athletes respond to Meyer so warmly, Lowe recalled later, was remarkable.

Meyer continued: "That means I know how to make a seventeen-hour drive to spend a two-hour home visit with a recruit and his family, and then get back in the car and make a seventeen-hour drive back home. If I had not coached forty years in small colleges, I probably wouldn't have developed the toughness to successfully negotiate the past ten months."

Meyer reached into the left breast pocket of his shirt and pulled out the small blue-and-gold laminated card that Wooden had given him, on which was typeset a couple of hundred words, including these: DAD'S SEVEN POINT CREED.

Holding up the card, Meyer said, "Yesterday, I was fortunate enough to visit with Coach John Wooden, and he gave me this card with guidance that his father gave to him upon his graduation from grade school. One of his dad's favorite pieces of advice was the following: Don't whine, don't complain, and don't make excuses.

"Every time I've gone to rehab workouts, these three statements have slapped me right in the face, as I glance around the room and see that everyone doing their rehab with me has it much tougher than I do.

"The *F* word has been used, unfortunately, highly in our society and the world today, and we use it in our basketball program, also. Our *F* words are 'faith,' 'family,' and 'friends.'"

There was loud clapping in the Nokia Theatre. "Faith that God . . ." The clapping had overwhelmed his words, and he stopped, for a moment. "Faith that God has a reason for sparing my life at this time, so I can try to serve others for a few more years.

"Family, such as my wife, Carmen, and our children, Jerry, Brooke, and Brittney, who have given me constant concern, care, and prayer. I would not be here tonight if my wife of forty-two years hadn't devoted her entire time to totally bringing me back from where I was.

"Friends, like our current team at Northern State University Wolves, all the former players from Northern State, Lipscomb University, and Hamline University, and coaches from all over the country who encouraged me with letters, emails, phone calls, and visits, and spent nights sitting with me all night long so that my wife could rest, so she could stay up the next day and make all of the big decisions.

"I've learned from this odyssey that peace is not the absence of troubles, trials, and torment but calm in the midst of them."

The audience fell silent. He had their full attention.

"I first met Coach Jim Valvano at a Nike clinic we were speaking at in San Francisco. When I sat in the hospitality room with him, he showed me how one human being could speak, tell jokes, laugh, and entertain us all for an hour without ever breathing. The man lived each moment to the fullest. He was high on life. He was the kind of guy who never wasted an at-bat. He always swung from the heels for the fences, and he never got cheated— not one time. And you know, that's the way I would like to live the rest of my life, and I think you would too.

"Jim Valvano achieved every goal he set for himself in life and in his career as a coach. When he reached the end of his run on this earth, he set one last goal: find a cure for cancer. And with all of us helping the Jimmy V. Foundation, I think he'll nail that one too. Thank you."

Those seated in the first rows rose to their feet immediately, and the others in the theater followed like a wave. Don Meyer had taught in small gymnasiums and small classrooms at small schools, and in this moment, that work and his excruciating fight back from the accident were honored. Thunderously.

Meyer pushed his walker offstage, Lowe at his side. "You killed it, Coach," Lowe said.

Carmen Meyer stood and clapped, and smiled. "Well," she said, taking a deep breath, "I'm glad that that's over with." Behind the curtains and immediately after the show, there were photos taken with Meyer holding the tall, silver ESPY trophy before everybody headed off to the after-party. Jerry Meyer pushed his father, now in his wheelchair, through a small alley that had been built for this event, a place where the athletes could walk to the reception without having to pass directly through the crowd of fans. As Don Meyer rolled past, a man leaned over the gate and extended a hand to the coach—Jeff Kent, who was in his first summer of retirement after playing seventeen years in the major leagues. He had never met Meyer, but after the coach's speech, he felt he needed to. Meyer, whose first love was baseball, immediately deflected Kent's praise about the speech—"I'm a lot more comfortable on a basketball court than I am speaking here," he told the ballplayer—and started talking about how much he had enjoyed watching Kent play. The conversation would stick with Kent, who, many months later, could recite almost word for word what was said.

After Jerry found a corner at the party where his father and the family could settle in, the other guests approached him to talk about his speech. But mostly Don Meyer spent the time with his friends and family; he sat and talked with Tomlinson and Hutcheson, his former players, for hours. The ESPYs had been a great time for all of them, Brittney said to the others. "We've got to find a way to get back here," she joked, "even if we have to push Dad off a cliff."

They left the party at one A.M., and at four A.M., Don Meyer rolled through the lobby of the Millennium to get a van back to the airport. The Meyers wanted an early start on their journey back to Aberdeen.

The day before Meyer's speech, his college friend Ron Vlasin had called, and Meyer mentioned that he was in Los Angeles. "What are you doing out there?" Vlasin asked.

"I don't know. ESPN has some kind of award thing going on," Meyer responded, and then changed the subject. On Sunday, July 19, Vlasin saw an advertisement for the ESPYs.

"Maybe that's what Don was talking about," Vlasin said to his wife, and so they turned on the television, unsure whether Meyer might receive some sort of award.

In Aberdeen that night, as the show began, another set of kids got settled in for the start of a week at the Northern State basketball camp. The Northern State players wanted to see the broadcast of the ESPYs to see their coach. But Meyer kept them at work until about nine thirty P.M., before the last half hour of the show, and when he released them from their evening's responsibilities, the players raced out of the Barnett Center, speeding out of the parking lot to see if they might catch a glimpse of Meyer. They had no real sense of how the night had gone for him because, of course, he really hadn't talked about it.

Brett Newton, one of the players who had tended to Meyer in

The Meyer family on the red carpet at the ESPYs.

the moments after his crash, had made a point not to watch any of the shows about Meyer's accident; he just didn't want to be reminded. But he wanted to watch the speech with just a couple of teammates from Northern State. As he listened, Newton thought: *How lucky have I been to hear him every day.*

Vlasin was stunned to see his old friend's speech, and he cried on hearing his words. Michael Snyder, the doctor who had happened upon the accident site because of a detour, watched in his home, full of admiration for Meyer and his words. Mindy Voss, the nurse who had grown close to the Meyers during the coach's rehab, watched and thought of the Alan Jackson CD they had listened to together.

Twelve hours later, after Meyer's speech was posted on YouTube, Rob Browne, one of Meyer's former players from David Lipscomb, sat in front of a laptop computer screen in Novosibirsk, a town in Siberia, where Browne worked at a youth camp for orphans. Browne watched the ceremony with his wife and children and other volunteers, and he felt the reaction of others in the room. How remarkable, Browne thought, that the essence of what made Meyer so extraordinary had reached to the other side of the world, in this little town in Russia. He watched the speech over and over, in tears.

Two months later, an episode of Terrell Owens's reality show, *The T.O. Show,* aired on VH1, and Carter Finley, Meyer's fifteen-year-old granddaughter, watched in her room. The drama on this episode centered around the wedding of Owens's agent, and at the conclusion of the ceremony, the microphone was passed to the wide receiver. "Every year around this time I'm already preparing for the football season," Owens said to the gathering. "What really keeps me going through the tough times are what I call the three Fs—my faith, my family, and my friendships. . . ."

Carter went to the family room, exclaiming, "You will not believe what Terrell Owens just said on his show—he just ripped off Grandpa's ESPY speech!"

An email went out, and was circulated among Meyer's former players, who batted this back and forth like a Greek chorus. One player noted that this might actually be considered one of Meyer's greatest achievements. "It could be the first time on record," the ex-player noted, "that Terrell Owens listened to a coach."

CHAPTER 18

Don Meyer was the worst fisherman that Ron Vlasin had ever seen. Years before Meyer's accident, Vlasin and Meyer had gone out on Lake McConaughy, Nebraska's largest body of water. Shortly after the two men had dropped their lines, Meyer asked Vlasin a question about the high school basketball team that Vlasin coached. With his back to Meyer, Vlasin started answering the question, keeping his voice low for fear of disturbing the fish. After a few minutes, Vlasin had glanced over at Meyer at the other side of the boat and saw that his friend had put down his rod, had pulled out a notebook, and was writing everything that Vlasin said.

But Vlasin found a different Don Meyer in the summer of 2009. The Meyers had never really done much in the way of vacations through the years, but this summer, after the basketball camps ended, they drove to Colorado to see Carmen's parents and, on the way back, visited with Ron and Terri Vlasin. On one sunny day, they all went fishing. Meyer initially declined to throw a line in the water, choosing instead to take the wheel of the boat. "Captain Meyer reporting for duty," he said. But one look at four poles dangling over the side of the boat all curled from the weight of fish, and Meyer had grabbed a rod, reeling in a white bass. "Nothing to this," he said dryly.

In the course of the day of fishing, Meyer turned to Vlasin and told him about something that he had done the year after Vlasin left Northern Colorado. The two had played baseball and basketball together. But Vlasin had signed to play professional baseball after his junior year at Northern Colorado, while Meyer had remained in school. As they sat in the boat on that summer day, Meyer told his friend that he had specifically asked for Vlasin's number 14 jersey because of how much he admired his friend. "Even though it was a little small for me," Meyer added.

Vlasin was surprised at how relaxed Meyer was; this was the longest passage of hours he had ever seen his friend with his mind away from basketball.

The Meyers continued meandering eastward, back toward Aberdeen, with their last stop in Sturgis, South Dakota, to see Tom and Cathie Anderson, the parents of Casey Anderson. Meyer walked through the door of the Andersons' house and said emphatically, "Okay, where's the sunroom? And where's your one-eyed dog?" The Meyers and Andersons went to dinner—the Andersons appreciating the visit this first summer after their youngest son's death.

A few days after the Meyers' vacation ended, Vlasin got something in the mail: a picture from Meyer, from the ESPYs, with a note written on it.

Ron: You're the older brother I never had.

Vlasin framed the picture from his friend and hung it on his wall.

Don Meyer would write a lot of notes the first year after his accident; it was a time for him to say things he wanted to say, to be with people he cared about, to reach out.

Rick Byrd, the head coach at Belmont in Nashville, had been Meyer's coaching nemesis for years. There had been years when Belmont struggled to compete with Meyer's teams, but under Byrd, Belmont's program got stronger and inflicted some crushing defeats—most notably the game in 1989 when Joe Behling scored fifty-eight points in Lipscomb's gym to end the season for a Bisons team that had only lost one game before then. Byrd's approach to his work was very different from that of Meyer. During the basketball season, he prepared intensely and recruited aggressively; but in the summer, when Meyer and the Lipscomb players were engrossed in operating the nation's largest basketball camps, Byrd would relax, playing golf, playing with his growing daughters. They were both successful men, with different styles.

Meyer had bumped into a mutual friend of his and Byrd's in the summer of 2009, and he reached for a pen and the first sheet of paper he could find—it was pink—and in his flowing handwriting he jotted down a note that he asked be delivered to Byrd:

> *Rick:*
> *Thank you for all of the nice things you have said about me.*
> *You taught me the true meaning of class and honor. You had demons to fight like all of us and you did it gracefully.*

I love you, Rick. You were always someone who made all around them better for associating with you.

Your friend,

Don

Jackie Witlock had worked for Northern State in a support position with the athletic department, and in the aftermath of Meyer's accident, she had worked closely with the players and helped Carmen. Meyer did not remember much from his days in the hospital, and so he had asked others about what had been done on his behalf.

Late in the summer of 2009, Jackie Witlock got a letter in the mail that included a reference to her husband.

Jackie:

Last night, I overheard Carmen reading a speech she will present today.

I heard your name mentioned several times.

It was all about the events that unfolded the night of the wreck. I did not know all that you did to comfort Carmen. There is much that I still do not know about that night.

In several ways, you helped to comfort my wife, my family, and make it possible for me to have a chance at more time on this earth with them.

I thank you and respect you for who you are . . .

And I love you and Woody,

Don

Jonathan Stone, the doctor who had worked with Meyer on his pain management at the Sioux Falls hospital, was walking past the nurses' station when he saw a man who seemed out of place. His office manager introduced him to the man, who was in charge of the hospital's foundation for raising money and had come to inform Stone that a donation had been made in his name, in honor of his work, by Don and Carmen Meyer. Stone, going through a difficult time in his own life, was overwhelmed.

In the summer of 2009, Meyer was fitted for an artificial leg, a prosthesis that fit imperfectly and sometimes led to infections in Little Buddy. Meyer got sore whenever he walked extensively, and joked about needing his pain medication. *Little Buddy is not happy,* he would say. But Meyer was no longer confined in the way that he had been right after the accident. He was cleared to drive, was happy to be able to walk with a cane, and relieved to be out of the wheelchair.

About a month after the ESPYs, Meyer parked in downtown Aberdeen, taking a visitor to Lager's Inn to visit Northern State's self-proclaimed number one fan, Nate Thompson, who was fifty-one years old, a cheerful South Dakotan with special needs; he was just finishing his shift for the day. Thompson happily chided Meyer again that Meyer had not mentioned him by name in his ESPYs speech. "I saw that, Don," Thompson said.

Since Meyer had started coaching, his programs usually were adopted by one or two special-needs adults—an element of his basketball program that was inspired by Carmen's brother J.D. Having played for Meyer and also having worked for him as an assistant coach, Jason Shelton thought that the inclusion of the special-needs adults in Meyer's programs served two purposes: First, Thompson and the others had a great time, and second, they reminded players that others thrived through greater challenges than the athletes faced.

At Northern State, Thompson tended to the ball rack on

game days, wearing a pair of jeans and a long-sleeved black shirt, shooting by himself at halftime until the Wolves players started to come out. Sometimes Meyer would ask him, in front of the players, what the Wolves needed to do, and Thompson's response was consistent: *You've got to work on your defense,* he would say, *work on your passing, and you got to hold your follow-through.* Jarod Markley, a local Special Olympics star in his early twenties, contributed a couple of things as well: It was his job to give hugs to each of the players, and to give the one-two-three count when the players gathered to stack their hands together before games.

On Sundays, the Meyers would pick up Nate Thompson at his apartment, near Lager's Inn, to take him to church and then to lunch. But on this day that Meyer stopped by Lager's Inn, Nate Thompson bore a couple of pieces of news. "Don, I made the goulash," Thompson said. He had a way of talking through his smile, so that each of his words sounded like a proud revelation.

Thompson had recently been the marshal at the Gypsy Day Parade—or, more accurately, he had been the honorary stand-in. Meyer had been picked as marshal, but he had recruited Thompson to sit in the convertible next to him and wave aggressively on his behalf. "Who do you like to wave to the most, Nate?" Meyer had asked him, like a lawyer leading his witness.

"The girls," Thompson had said, beaming.

Meyer laughed with Thompson as he told the story, and later in the day he shook with laughter again, sitting on a picnic table at the Brown County fair—a central location, between the rides and the agriculture barns, that gave him a chance to see a lot of friends. Meyer had running conversations with each of them. It was a different kind of summer; it was a different kind of year. There had been years when Carmen Meyer could barely get her husband to go out and do events, but Meyer was now much more open, his wife thought, much more relaxed.

The Meyers stopped by a local ice cream cone shop. Don Meyer's left leg was sore after a day of walking around on Little Buddy, so he asked Carmen to get some ice cream for him—a root beer float, he said with relish. One of the visitors ordered a triple-scoop chocolate cone, the other a sprawling banana split, and Carmen ordered a heaping creamie swirl for herself. For her husband, she brought back a thumb-sized cup better suited for samples at a grocery store; she was concerned about his diet.

Don Meyer stared down at the cup in mock anger and then stared at his wife. "So *that's* how it's going to be, eh?" he said, and then he laughed again.

Carmen Meyer felt that her relationship with Don had strengthened enormously since the accident. "It's so much better now," she said. "He's much more considerate of me and my activities, and my time." The time after the accident, she was convinced, had been a blessing for them.

Randy Baruth had spoken to him that summer and could hear his happiness. He seemed stronger, healthier. Baruth thought he was reloading, emotionally, for the upcoming basketball season. Meyer had a major competitive chip on his shoulder: The Northern State assistants had heard during the summer that other teams were using Meyer's physical condition and terminal illness against him in the recruiting wars. Friends believed that Meyer was champing at the bit for another season, and the Wolves looked to have a very good team—and a chance to be the kind of tough, physical team that Meyer loved.

The old intensity was back, and now that he could move with a cane, he could coach more readily. He seemed to be doing so well, Baruth thought, that you almost forgot the man had terminal cancer.

Four days after the night at the Brown County fair, the Meyers had an appointment to get the results of the scan from the previous week. The doctor held up his index finger and thumb to describe how much the largest tumor in Meyer's liver had grown—three-quarters of an inch to an inch—since his previous scan. The doctor told them he had never seen any carcinoid cancer grow that quickly, and recommended that Meyer begin a regimen of hormone shots, two a day for a week, in an effort to slow the manifestation of the cancer in his body. Perhaps the shots would help to treat the symptoms of the cancer, the doctor said, but it wasn't guaranteed.

As the Meyers pulled out of the parking lot, Carmen looked over and saw her husband tearing up.

On the first Friday of the 2009–2010 school year at Northern State University, members of the men's basketball team prepared for their annual retreat to the hunting lodge. The players waited in the parking lot, not sure exactly what would happen. Most of them had not been past the scene of the accident since that fateful day the year before. When Meyer had referred to the upcoming trip, he never mentioned that terrible day. They weren't sure if he would drive himself, or if somebody else would take the wheel.

Meyer pushed his walker out of the gym, slowly. The coach whose sense of humor ran from dry to bone-dry said drolly, "I want to let everyone know that I *won't* be making the drive this year."

The players laughed.

First-year graduate assistant Max Schuman would drive Meyer's van to the lodge with Meyer in the passenger seat. As they pulled out of the parking lot, Meyer explained flatly to Schuman, in case he didn't know, that this was the annual trip on which the accident had occurred the year before. Of course,

Schuman knew, but he didn't respond. Meyer never mentioned this again in the forty-mile journey.

For Newton and the Northern State players, the drive was quiet. Some of them noted the accident site, but few said anything. It was surreal to think about how that day had impacted their lives and how it changed the life of their coach, Don Meyer. It had been a day of rebirth. But in the lead car of the caravan, Meyer didn't talk about the accident.

He turned to Schuman, a twenty-five-year-old with a whole life ahead of him, someone who had been recommended as a graduate assistant by Vlasin. After finishing school, Schuman had worked selling vacation club memberships, and then started a home security company. But what Schuman really wanted to do was teach, and coach, and so he had moved to Aberdeen to work with a legendary coach.

Meyer settled into his seat for the journey and began asking the young man questions about his past and his dreams.

CHAPTER 19

The last season that Meyer would coach started badly. Less than two weeks into practice, Bojan Todorovic, who was expected to be a pivotal piece of Northern State's front line, tore a knee ligament in practice and would miss the rest of the season. Not long after that, point guard Brett Newton was sidelined with stress fractures and a tear of a knee tendon; he would not play for the final three months. With two of their most important players sidelined, the Wolves would struggle for consistency, and Meyer would struggle to coach at the level he expected of himself.

Two hours before Northern State opened the 2009–2010 season, Meyer asked one of his assistant coaches to close the door to his office so that he could dress. He pulled on a pair of dark blue slacks, first over his right leg and then over his prosthetic leg, which he now referred to as Roger Legge, named for an Aberdeen resident by that name.

Brad Christenson, an assistant coach for Meyer at Northern State, bent forward on one knee and, using two shoehorns, helped wedge the prosthesis inside a black shoe. After struggling for about five minutes, Christenson finally got the shoe to fit. "It takes a lot of work to get dressed now," said Meyer flatly.

Pushing himself up with his cane, Meyer got up and walked slowly and evenly out of the office. His assistant coaches felt that it was much easier for him to coach with Roger Legge than it had been when Meyer was in a wheelchair, and his players sensed that his energy from before the accident had been largely restored. They knew that cancer was growing inside of him, they recognized the small signs of his illness, and they knew, generally, that he was receiving hormone therapy. But Meyer never talked about it with them.

The Wolves met about forty-five minutes before that first game of the season, sitting in front of their gold lockers, under a large sign that read, THE STRENGTH OF THE PACK IS IN THE WOLF AND THE STRENGTH OF THE WOLF IS IN THE PACK. One by one, the starters delivered scouting reports for the others about the opponents they would guard, the Jamestown College Jimmies, an NAIA team that had bused about an hour to get to Aberdeen. Meyer stressed to them the importance of fundamentals and reminded them to maintain their intensity: "Plan, prepare, practice, and play just like you lost your last game."

The pregame session ended, and Meyer left the locker room with his cane. But when the game began, Meyer left his cane on the bench and, for the next two hours, limped back and forth in front of Northern State's bench, up and down, as he had always done. He shouted and cajoled and admonished his players; as he saw mistakes, he lifted the voice recorder he held in his left hand to make notes to himself about things that needed to be corrected.

And there were a lot of mistakes in the Wolves' first game: too many turnovers, a lack of flow with their offense. Northern State's practices were physical, the players aggressively working on their defense and rebounding, and sometimes it took some time for them to adjust this for games that were officiated; thus, they were whistled for twenty-nine fouls. They struggled with their passing game. But they rebounded well, at almost a two-to-one margin, and won, 93–74. After the coaches and players shook hands and began to move off the court, Nate Thompson handed Meyer his cane.

Not long after leaving the court, Meyer realized that he'd forgotten to take his pain medication. "We'll see how that goes," he said to a visitor, raising his eyebrows, knowing there would be discomfort.

Meyer drove home and went into the kitchen, where Carmen was pulling out plastic bowls of leftovers to heat him some dinner: barbecue and mashed potatoes. "What'd you think?" Carmen asked.

"Not very good," he said. "We've got to get better."

The sun was out the next day, a bright and cloudless morning. The Wolves had another game that night, after a two P.M. practice, and Meyer didn't have to go into the office until ten A.M.; he had slept in until after seven A.M. "It feels like a vacation," he said.

He sat in his living room chair, gazing at the proud blue jays out on the patio, who searched for the last remnants from an otherwise empty feeder, and the squirrels, who appeared to be fattened up for the winter, having found a way to circumvent the squirrel guard. So many people in Aberdeen spent their winters in Florida or Texas or Arizona to avoid the extreme cold. Meyer didn't want that, he had decided. He wanted to live here for the rest of his life.

The Wolves continued to struggle with turnovers in their second game, passing inefficiently. The next morning, Meyer took a seat in front of the players and told them he had been up late, thinking of ways to help with the team's passing game. "I'm going to prepare for every practice like this was going to be my last practice," he said.

Meyer challenged them to be ready, always. "When you get your chance," he said, raising his voice, "you've got to raise the level of intensity. You've got to raise the level of confidence. You've got to raise the level of excellence." The players wrote down the words in their notebooks, in ink.

After practice, Meyer sat at his desk, picked through emails, and mused about his future. "I pretty much made up my mind I'm going to coach as long as I live," he said. "I'm hoping I can coach these redshirt freshmen we have all the way through their eligibility, and that'd be five years. I hope I can live that long."

He paused for a moment and said, "Just when you've got it figured out, then your time is up."

Earlier in the fall of 2009, Jerry Meyer had flown to Aberdeen to spend time with his parents and help coach Wolves practice. A few weeks later, Brooke and Brittney had visited. For Brittney, it was the first time she had seen her father since the ESPYs, and Brooke had warned her that although their father was using Roger Legge and a cane, he was still very much hampered by his handicap.

Brittney knew that her father saw her as the comedian in the group, and on the trip to Aberdeen, she prepared herself in the same way that a comic might before a performance. She came through the door of her father's house with one-liners at the ready, surprising her sleeping father from behind and covering his eyes. "Guess who it is, Dad," she said, and he shook with laughter.

But it was more difficult for her than she let on. For Brittney, the days in the hospital with her father, hearing him speak to her with such feeling, had been deeply meaningful. Now, a year later, she almost wanted everything to go back to the way it had been before the accident. When he spoke to her with such openness, there was unwanted weight attached to his words. Cancer was attached to the words. After her father got the prosthetic leg, a sense of normalcy had been restored, a feeling that now he could move on with his life, the cancer seemingly dormant. But the news in August that his cancer had advanced had stunned them all.

On November 23, Meyer met with his doctor, who told him that his cancer hadn't grown much since his appointment in August. But Meyer's heart rate was at 40, and he was tired. The appointment ended, and he was drained. "I'm tired of fighting," he told Carmen.

She fought sadness. She told her daughters how much she appreciated her interaction with her husband, the way that he cared for her, the way they cared for each other—and now he was beset with a terminal illness.

Northern State lost six of their last seven games before the Christmas break, and Meyer told his assistant coaches that he was sure that this was his fault. The culture of the team seemed to have changed since the accident; Meyer was convinced that this was largely because he didn't have the energy to force the players to come together and commit themselves to one another, to work through the cliques that the staff felt had developed. His assistants tried to assure him that the problems were more about the particular mix of personalities on the team.

But Meyer had taught his players for decades about accountability, and as far as he was concerned, the struggles of this team were his responsibility. The players weren't meshing properly and he was the coach, and because the problem wasn't getting fixed, this was his fault.

Meyer was sure now that because he couldn't get on the court and challenge the players and confront them about their mistakes, his ability to teach was compromised. He wanted to be able to physically demonstrate for them how to work through a pick, how to chin a ball, how to throw a bounce pass. He wanted to work with them on their shot mechanics. But the reality was that he was crippled; he could not do those things leaning on a cane.

When the team traveled, he hated feeling that the players were waiting for him as he slowly moved around, whether it was onto a bus or into a hotel. He had hoped that the Northern players would seize the initiative and fill the leadership void themselves, and not require him to constantly demand, cajole, threaten, and harangue. When David Lipscomb won the national title in 1986, they had become a self-sustaining unit by the end of that season, capable of playing a game without coaching, he thought. But the Northern State players needed more, and he knew he couldn't provide it for them.

The Meyers went to Nashville for the Christmas break to visit their children, and Meyer spent a lot of the vacation—which was extended by a snowstorm that shut down the airport—in the large chair in Brooke's living room. On Christmas Eve, the major story in college sports was that Urban Meyer, the forty-five-year-old football coach at the University of Florida (who was not related to Don Meyer), was taking a leave of absence, essentially because of exhaustion. The news gnawed at Don Meyer as he sat in the chair, and he made the obvious points out loud for others in the room: Urban Meyer was much younger than Don Meyer, and he *wasn't* fighting a terminal illness, and yet the relentless demands of coaching had worn Urban Meyer down.

Nevertheless, just before he returned to the Wolves' practice a few days later, on December 29, 2009, Don Meyer told Carmen that he wanted to coach *two* more years. His tone was strong.

Practice did not go well. His players seemed to be drifting emotionally, and in the past, he could have moved onto the court, shown them a shooting drill, and made enough shots to make it clear to them that he knew what he was talking about; Philip Hutcheson could remember Meyer shooting nonstop for thirty minutes as he lectured at David Lipscomb, making basket after basket. In the past, he would have loudly challenged their toughness; he could have confronted the corrosive problem of cliques that had beset the Northern team. But now he didn't have use of his left leg and he was out of breath as he moved slowly around the court with his walker. Whether because of himself or them, Meyer was not reaching them, and he recognized it.

Randy Baruth had moved on to serve as an assistant coach at Division I Colorado State during the summer, but he and Meyer talked frequently about the team over the phone. In the past, Meyer and Baruth agreed, the players had feared him, and this fear drove them into practicing and executing the way Meyer wanted. Now the players felt sorry for him, Baruth thought, because of Meyer's leg and because of his cancer.

Don Meyer called Brittney, his voice sounding as strong and as resolute as it had been earlier in the day when he had told Carmen he would coach two more years. "I think it's time to step away from coaching," he told his daughter. Brittney knew how tired he was and how tough of a season the Wolves were having. But she had assumed that he would coach until his last moment:

She could picture him having a fatal heart attack during the course of a game. On one hand, his family was relieved that he was seriously considering leaving coaching, and on the other hand, the decision was almost incomprehensible to them.

At three A.M. on New Year's Eve, Don Meyer could not sleep. This was the decision that he had always feared. He had been convinced for years that the idea of walking away from coaching would be emotionally crushing, because he would be stepping away from something that had been at the center of his life and committing himself to moving forward into an abyss. For almost five decades, he had been working from a daily planner that was structured around basketball, and now he knew that he could no longer coach.

Meyer pulled out a yellow pad and started to write out the letter of resignation that he would give to the Northern State president, eventually. And he was surprised by how good he felt about it.

"I have never felt like this in my life," he said over the phone, a few hours later. "I have total peace of mind. It's the right time. I always wondered how I would know when it's the right time. Well, I know. It's the right time. . . . You've got to be willing to kill yourself to do this job. The job of motivating kids, to pull kids through things they need to learn, can only be done at tremendous emotional and physical costs. I'm just too tired to fight it anymore. I'm not going to kill myself.

"I feel bad in a way, because you don't want to be a quitter. But I'm just not going to kill myself."

A few weeks later, Northern State president James Smith met with Meyer and Brenda Dreyer privately. Dreyer looked over at Meyer and saw that he looked wiped out, his face drawn.

"I'm sorry to do this to the school, but I just can't do this anymore," Meyer said. He was stepping down as coach.

And he went on to explain how much the travel—the long bus rides—wore on him. Smith apologized and said that if Northern State were a Division I school, they could fly to games.

They talked about how Meyer's decision would be revealed. First and foremost, he didn't want any announcement made until right near the end of the season, because he did not want to be at the center of some maudlin retirement tour in which he was constantly honored by other schools. He had wanted to tell Smith of his decision as soon as possible so that the head of the school would know that he had to find a basketball coach, but he did not want to be the center of attention for the next eight weeks.

Part of Meyer's fear about leaving coaching was that he didn't know exactly what would be next for him—and the idea of not having work was frightening to someone who had grown up on a Nebraska farm always believing that hard work was life. He had asked Brooke if she thought that he might be able to do some consulting work with basketball programs, and she tried to assure him. Leaving his job, he mused to a friend, would be like a funeral. Inactivity was perhaps the thing that he feared the most.

Smith settled that issue quickly. "We want you to stay here, to help," he said, and he explained how Meyer could aid with the school's fundraising and other events. Meyer would have an office in the primary administration building, and Smith had just the place in mind.

There was concern among his friends and family about whether Meyer would get through the season. In January, tests showed that the growth in his cancerous tumors had slowed, but he still did not feel well. Meyer's resting heart rate had always been low, but there was a night when it fell to 35 beats a minute. Meyer would stand throughout games without the use of a cane, but he felt faint at times, as if he could not get enough oxygen.

His mortality weighed on him. He showed a visitor a list of the songs he wanted played at his funeral, and with a smile, Meyer mentioned that he wanted to be buried in the suit that he had worn at the ESPYs covering the upper half of his body—and for the lower half, he wanted the tie-dyed underwear that his grandson Zev had made for him. "Maybe we can get a casket that only opens at the top," Meyer mused.

But he did make it to the end of the basketball season. After a morning practice on February 22, Meyer told the players to meet in the locker room. The room went silent when Meyer said that the school would announce his retirement in half an hour. He explained to the players that he thought that Northern State's recruiting was affected by his lack of stamina, and that he thought the players needed more hands-on instruction. As Meyer mentioned that he could no longer demonstrate to them, his voice cracked; he told them that he loved them.

Meyer, seemingly trying to end the meeting while he still had his composure, finished his remarks and moved toward the door—and stumbled. Casey Becker, a junior forward who had loved playing for Meyer, caught him with the help of another player before the coach fell.

Meyer righted himself and walked out; behind him, the players remained in silence, except for the weeping of Becker and others.

The Wolves needed to win their final regular season game on February 27, 2010, at home to qualify for a postseason tournament.

*Don Meyer speaks to the players for the last time
on his final day as a coach.*

Before the game, a marble bust of Meyer was unveiled at center court. Jerry Meyer had made the trip, as had Brooke and Brittney, and Chase and Carter Finley, Brittney's children. So had Meyer's mother, Edna, and his sister, Nancy. Meyer's face was cast in the same stoic look that many players had felt for years. John Schwan, the father of former Northern State player Kyle Schwan, had sponsored the bust, and spoke. Everybody in the Wachs Arena crowd of almost six thousand was standing. "There is nobody that we've ever met who is harder on themselves than Don Meyer," said Schwan. "When I think of Don, I think of a man unafraid to lead. I think of a man unafraid to believe in and stand for something at the highest level. I think of a man who is unafraid of criticism. I think of a man unafraid to love. Coach Meyer has left a mark—his work. I call it perseverance."

The Wolves had led by four points with seven minutes to play, but were overwhelmed down the stretch. Don Meyer's career as a coach ended with 923 wins; this was the 324th loss.

The crowd remained to hear him speak. "There's nothing like coaching a team," he said. "There's nothing that will replace that, ever. The thing I hope is that we can all be a team, in this community, to do the things that need to be done, to keep Aberdeen growing."

Meyer's voice was steady. "I want to thank my family," he continued. "Carmen has done everything to keep me going. I've gone in her office and looked at the life insurance policies, and I don't know why she's doing it. I'm worth more dead than alive."

Those in the crowd laughed. He had them; they had him.

"But I wanted to have this chance to tell you guys that you're special," he said. "There are people who prayed for us and really cared for us. It was a wonderful thing to see. And the people in Aberdeen and the surrounding community are just great people. You're not fake, you're not phony; you're real. When you say something, you mean it, and you follow up what you say.

"I want to thank God for giving me the family I have, and the teams and players and coaches I've been able to work with.

"And I want to thank Him most of all for letting me live long enough to coach so many, many games and teams and to meet so many wonderful people. Thank you."

Don Meyer walked off to a final ovation.

Brenda Dreyer showed Meyer what would become his new office. Room No. 101 was at least three times larger than Meyer's office at the Barnett Center, with a large closet and enough room for a desk and a couch. He talked about where he might arrange the furniture. He talked about where he might hang pictures and store stuff.

A winter storm had just passed through Aberdeen, and the campus at Northern State was blanketed in white. Meyer looked out the window—a perfect window, because it looked out onto the common area of the campus, where students walked with hope and expectations and dreams, where Meyer could see life going forward.

At that moment, though, a couple of members of the school's maintenance staff guided snowblowers along the sidewalk, through the drifts. Meyer's right eyebrow curled upward.

"Hey!" he barked through the closed window. "You missed a spot!"

ACKNOWLEDGMENTS

In reporting about Coach Don Meyer for ESPN and for this book, I made six trips to Aberdeen, South Dakota, in the course of sixteen months, and the place reminded me a lot of where I grew up in central Vermont—and it was easy to see why the Meyers have liked it so much there. The people were warm and open, and were always there to help as I worked on this book.

In particular, many thanks to these folks in the Northern State University community: Randy Baruth, Brenda Dreyer, Jackie Witlock, Matt Hammer, Derik Budig, Brad Christenson, and Ryan Hilgemann. Their memories and thoughts were invaluable in understanding a man they respect and love.

The Northern State University basketball players were always helpful: Kyle Schwan, Brett Newton, Casey Becker, Kevin

Ratzsch, Bojan Todorovic, Marty Gregor, Tom Giesen, Mitch Boeck, Derek Hoellein, Tramel Barnes, Alex Thomas, Jordan King, Rob Thomas, Collin Pryor, and others.

Many thanks to Bob Olson, Meghan Baruth, Jacque Scoby, Max Schuman, and Dan Magrino, and NSU president James Smith for their assistance. Some others from the Aberdeen community who made time for interviews: Don and Reva Carda, Cindy Kraft, Harley Mohr, Nate Reede, Dick Ward, Greg Wieker, and Dean Zimmerman. John Papendick of the *Aberdeen American News* was always the perfect person to bounce stuff off, and he helped with an important picture. Tom and Cathie Anderson spoke openly about the worst nightmare for any parents.

I was fortunate enough to have already known a lot of the players from David Lipscomb College (Lipscomb University, as it is now known), and among those, Philip Hutcheson, Jason Shelton, Rob Browne, Brent High, and Richard Taylor shared their memories. Barb Anderson, Meyer's longtime assistant, was among the first I spoke with after Coach Meyer's accident, and she provided great support. Old friend Mark McGee helped track down some history. Steve Smiley, who played for Coach Meyer at Northern State, wrote a book called *Playing for Coach Meyer*, and I drew valuable insight and stories from his pages.

I had always had high regard for Wade Tomlinson when I covered him as a player, but now, in working on this project, I found him and Jennifer Tomlinson to be inspirational souls, as they talked so movingly about coping with an unthinkable tragedy.

I am grateful to many others who were interviewed for the book: Trintje Bauer, Rick Byrd, Tim Corbin, Sheriff Kurt Hall, Jeff Kent, Bob Knight, Jerry Krause, Rob Lowe, George Sage, Tubby Smith, Dr. Michael Snyder, Bob Starkey, Trooper Carl Stearns, Dr. David Strand, Dr. Jonathan Stone, Pat Summitt, Senator John Thune, Ron Vlasin, Mindy Voss, and John Wooden.

My first trips to Aberdeen were made as a part of an ESPN E:60 crew that put together a long-form piece on Don Meyer. Thanks to producer Heather Lombardo, directors of photography Brad Milsap and Jeff Saunders, J. Scott Buckley (key sound), Dave McCoy (sound), Mark Mostad (sound and third camera), Tim Ryan (gaffer), and Dave Fleer (field producer). And thanks to the folks in Bristol who helped Heather shape the piece in post-production: editors Rob Labay, Joe Canali, and Warren Wolcott.

Andy Tennant and Robert Abbott, the head honchos at E:60, embraced this piece, as did my immediate bosses: John Skipper, Norby Williamson, Vince Doria, John Walsh, and Gary Belsky. Gary Hoenig has had incredible patience as I waded through this project, among others. Dr. Gary Clark and Stephania Bell helped with medical questions.

Hannah Deming, my much older sister, somehow managed to find time in her very busy schedule to provide immediate feedback, editing, and encouragement; she was an engine for this book. Dick and Louise Schwingel had the patience to work through the roughest first drafts, and their work is all over this book. Others chimed in with the needed thoughts and criticism as well: Sam Lincoln, Mark Simon, Greg Boro, Amelia Lincoln, Ed McGregor, Jon Scher, and Mark Schuman.

Many thanks to my agent, Chris Calhoun, who always saw this project as I did.

Jonathan Jao, my editor at Ballantine, enthusiastically embraced Don Meyer's story and made it his own, shaping the manuscript with ideas and thoughts. Jessie Waters and Kelly Chian helped to steer this through the process, making it better.

I obviously could not have attempted to write a story as intimate as this without having had incredible access to the extended Meyer family—particularly Carmen Meyer and Jerry,

Brooke, and Brittney, who all patiently answered many questions in person and over the phone, and in many emails.

And thanks to Lisa, Sydney, and Jake, for sharing their love (and patience).

I first met Don Meyer when I was twenty-four years old and a first-year reporter at the *Nashville Banner*. My winter assignment was to cover the city's NAIA league colleges, including David Lipscomb, where he coached. My own experience in getting to know him was similar to that of others: He seemed gruff at first, obtuse. He actually reminded me, right off the bat, of an old, bald farmer who lived near my family's farm in Randolph Center, Vermont, a man named Hank Huett who could be blunt and tough—and who could always be counted on if your tractor got stuck.

Meyer's practices were always open to the public, and so, once or twice a week, I would sit in and watch and listen. When the team met in a classroom before or after practices, I would take a seat in the back. The underlying message that I heard him present to his players—that every single day provided you with the opportunity to pursue excellence or not—resonated with me from a young age. From time to time he'd ask me a question about baseball, which I covered for the *Banner,* or about working as a reporter.

"Do you love what you do?" he asked, in such a way that it felt like he was testing the depth of my soul.

Once I mentioned to one of the Lipscomb assistant coaches the high level of frustration I felt with colleagues who showed up late for work, and wondered aloud how much longer I could work there, given the lack of punctuality in some corners of our department. The assistant must have mentioned this to Meyer, because about three days later I got a card in the mail from the Lipscomb basketball office:

Buster—
Patience.
—Coach Meyer

Lipscomb's rivalry with Belmont College at that time was extremely intense. Both schools were nationally ranked, but while Lipscomb was the established power—like the New York Yankees, on that level of basketball—Belmont was a program on the rise. David Lipscomb was a Church of Christ school, and Belmont was a Baptist school, the two campuses just two miles apart on the same street. Playing basketball was a year-round deal at David Lipscomb, between the season and the camps, but at Belmont, the players mostly relaxed, playing recreational pickup games in the summer. Belmont's coach, Rick Byrd, would spend his summers playing golf; he had a life outside of basketball. For Meyer and the Lipscomb players, basketball was life, and life was basketball. They played for championships in both years I covered the programs, and there was so much interest in the Lipscomb-Belmont games in 1989–90 that one of them was moved to the 15,300-seat arena at Vanderbilt—and sold out. And what was striking to me, as a young reporter, was that both programs seemed to have good people.

Years later, after I had accumulated more than a decade in the business, I was often asked: What was your favorite event to cover?

I had been fortunate enough to cover the Orioles for *The Baltimore Sun* when Cal Ripken broke Lou Gehrig's consecutive-game record. I had covered the Yankees through three championship seasons while at *The New York Times*. I had covered the incredible 2001 World Series, which, in the first weeks after 9/11, was a moving experience. But the most fun I ever had, I would always say, was covering the rivalry between Belmont and David Lipscomb for two seasons back in Nashville.

I had kept in touch with Coach Meyer after leaving Nashville.

He always loved to ask me about particular baseball players and what made them tick as competitors. On the day after his accident, I got an email from a friend from Tennessee who knew of my friendship with Coach Meyer.

A week after the accident, Meyer left me a phone message. "Buster," he said in a weak and gravelly voice, "I need to catch you up on this crap."

We spent a lot of time together as I worked on the story of his return to basketball, and on this book. Along the way, he was patient with my insistence that he would have to talk about himself, which is something he does not like to do.

On January 29, 2010, I spent the afternoon at his house going through the hundreds and hundreds of letters that he had received from coaches, some of which appear in Chapter 8. Meanwhile, Don and Carmen Meyer spoke with a doctor about his cancer. An hour or so before Northern's game that night, I saw him at the gym and mentioned to him how remarkable some of the letters were, and that I had picked out some of them to use in the book.

Northern State performed terribly in the game that night. Coach Meyer had looked tired during the game, moving up and down in front of the Northern State bench without use of his cane, and this was probably one of the worst games one of Meyer's teams had ever played. He was nothing less than devastated—frustrated by the decisions of his players, but also angry because he felt he was powerless to change the way they were playing, to coach them in a way they needed to be coached.

I carried some of his stuff out of the office to his car, and he continued to gripe about how badly the game had gone, how he felt like he couldn't coach the way he wanted to anymore. He paused for a moment and drew back his shoulders. "It feels like sometimes I can't catch my breath," he said.

His van had been parked in the handicap spot directly in front of the building, and he moved slowly toward his car. "You know, I thought I would get one thousand victories by the time I was sixty-five years old," he said. "We were reeling them off at Lipscomb, thirty-five to forty a year, and you can really pile them up really fast that way. I really thought I would get to a thousand."

I had never heard him talk about his career victory totals before; neither had his Northern State players, even on the night he broke the record. I suspected that the reason he was leery of talking about it out loud, for all the world to hear, was that he thought it might come off as selfish. I thought it was just a reflection of his competitiveness, which was as inherent in him as the baldness that he made fun of. The man did not seem to take a breath without striving for something; of course he set goals.

And at that moment, standing in the parking lot in the sub-zero weather of Aberdeen, South Dakota, he referred to the fact that he was on the Basketball Hall of Fame ballot in 2010.

"If I get in," he said, "I'm going to talk about the small college coaches." Meyer mentioned several names. "They should be in the Hall of Fame. Because they're coaching basketball and what's most important to them is that they did it the right way."

When we got back to the Meyers' home, he was in no mood to sleep. "What else did you see?" he asked again, and so we talked about the game, about the team, about his plans.

The doctor, he said, had provided some news that seemed to be encouraging. The cancer tumors in his intestine had not really grown since November. "So that's a good sign," he said.

What he did not tell me then was that there were more tumors. At the time he was originally diagnosed, the doctors had explained that as the carcinoid cancer spread, his organs would begin to fail. His heart rate had fallen to 35 beats per minute the previous week, and he had passed out in his office.

He had felt faint during the game that the Wolves had just

played, he said, and he had had a hard time catching his breath. "I just need to get to the end of the season," he said. "I don't want to quit. I just want to get to the end of the season."

Coach Meyer bounced around in his conversation, shifting from his health to his concerns about his players to the next coach, and in the midst of all that, he held up a white sheet of paper that had four lines written on it. "These are the songs that I want played at my funeral," he said.

"Why would you do that today?" I asked.

"Yeah, I tell you, I've got peace of mind over this decision [to retire]," he said, and he never did answer my question.

It was past one A.M. I had mentioned to him several times that he needed to get to bed. He told me he wanted to work on the book, to answer questions that we hadn't gotten to. I told him we could do that another time. It was very late, I had a plane to catch in five hours, and he looked exhausted; his day had started twenty-one hours before.

Coach Meyer was still wearing his jacket and his ski cap that he had worn back from the gym to keep him warm. He started to gather his stuff, and I got up off the couch. "Hold on," he said. "I'm going to give you a hug."

I'd had the same experience that others had, after the accident. For that, and for his time and his thoughts, I owe Coach Meyer many thanks.

ABOUT THE AUTHOR

BUSTER OLNEY is a senior writer at *ESPN The Magazine* and an analyst for ESPN's *Baseball Tonight*. He joined ESPN in June 2003 to cover baseball for all ESPN entities, including ESPN Radio, ESPNEWS, and *SportsCenter*. He currently writes a popular baseball blog for ESPN.com. He arrived at ESPN after six years at *The New York Times* covering the Mets (1997) and the Yankees (1998–2001). Olney has also authored the *New York Times* bestseller *The Last Night of the Yankee Dynasty: The Game, the Team, and the Cost of Greatness* (HarperCollins, 2004), a book about the Paul O'Neill/Tino Martinez Yankees dynasty of 1996–2001.

ABOUT THE TYPE

The text of this book was set in Legacy, a typeface family designed by Ronald Arnholm and issued in digital form by ITC in 1992. Both its serifed and unserifed versions are based on the original type created by the French punchcutter Nicholas Jenson in the late fifteenth century. While Legacy tends to differ from Jenson's original in its proportions, it maintains much of the latter's characteristic modulations in stroke.